Bible Detectives
1 Samuel

FUN BIBLE STUDIES USING PUZZLES & STORIES

Written by Marianne Ross
Illustrated by Ron Wheeler

Cover Design by Daniel van Straaten
Printed and bound by Bell and Bain, Glasgow

Published by Christian Focus Publications,
Geanies House, Fearn, Tain, Ross-shire, IV20 1TW, Scotland, UK.
www.christianfocus.com email: info@christianfocus.com
ISBN: 978-1-84550-569-1

Introduction

Hello, we are Jess and Harry. Welcome to our investigation. Let's learn about a book in the Bible called 1 Samuel.

1 Samuel is in the Old Testament. It is full of adventures, but has some sad stories too. You will meet lots of different people. With Click's help you will have fun solving the puzzles and you will discover more about God.

Bible Fact File

There are 39 books in the Old Testament and 27 books in the New Testament. The Old Testament books were written before God's Son, Jesus Christ, came to earth as a baby. The New Testament was written after Jesus' death and resurrection.

But who is Jesus Christ and what exactly happened to him? Well, before we start Click has downloaded one or two Jesus facts.

He was crucified. Jesus was put to death by the Roman authorities and by the Jewish religious leaders. He was nailed to a cross and left to die. However, his death was all part of a greater plan by God, his Father, to save sinners from the punishment of sin and to give them eternal life.

Jesus rose from the dead. The word people use to describe this event is Resurrection. Jesus Christ came back to life through the power of God. He defeated death and sin. King David was also an ancestor of Jesus - but because Jesus is the King of kings and the Son of God Jesus is sometimes referred to as King David's greater son.

Different people wrote the books of the Bible - some were kings and warriors, some were prophets and preachers, others were fishermen and one was even a doctor. But all of these writers were inspired by God - so although their minds came up with the words and their hands wrote the words - it is God who is the real author of the Bible.

Follow the wiggly lines and you will match up each author with one of the Bible verses that they wrote.

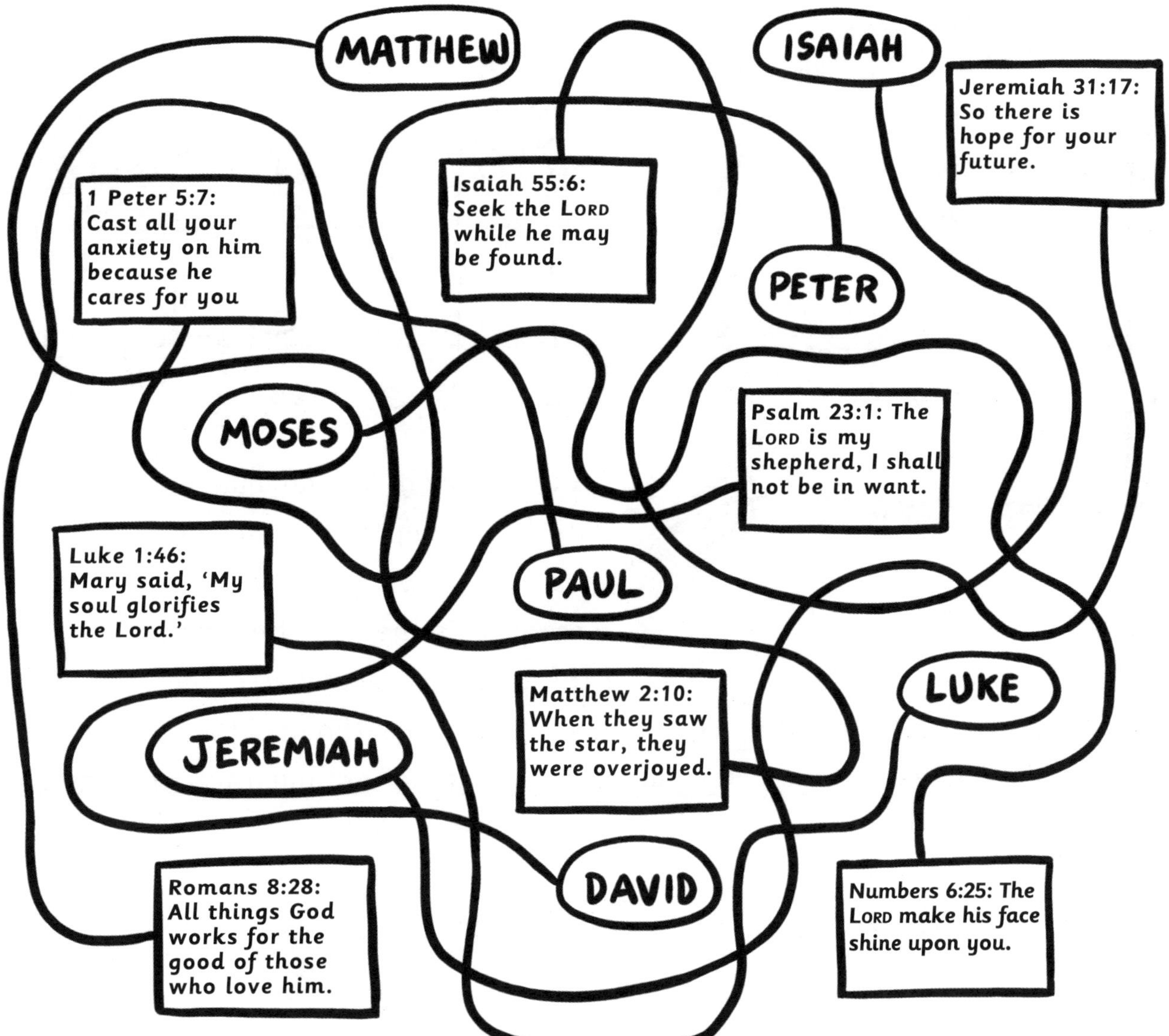

Now let's go on to find out more about who this guy Samuel really was. There are more puzzles to solve and questions to answer. Let's go!

1. Hannah and Elkanah

Click wants to help us discover what happened before Samuel was born. Samuel's father, Elkanah, had two wives; one was called Hannah and the other Peninnah. Peninnah had lots of children, but Hannah had none and this made her very sad. But just before we go on, have a look at the following Bible fact - which will explain things that you need to know.

Elkannah had two wives which was against God's law. Many people in Israel were living like the ungodly nations around them and did not follow God's commands.

Elkanah lived at Ramah and every year he went with his family to worship the LORD at Shiloh. Eli and his two sons, Hophni and Phinehas, were priests there. After the sacrificial meal Hannah went away to pray for a son. If the LORD answered her prayer she promised to give her son back to the LORD. Eli saw her praying and thought that she was drunk. Hannah explained that she had not had too much to drink, but that she was greatly troubled. Use the funny faces to discover what Eli said next.

a e i o u

G_ _n p_ _c_ _nd m_y th_ G_d

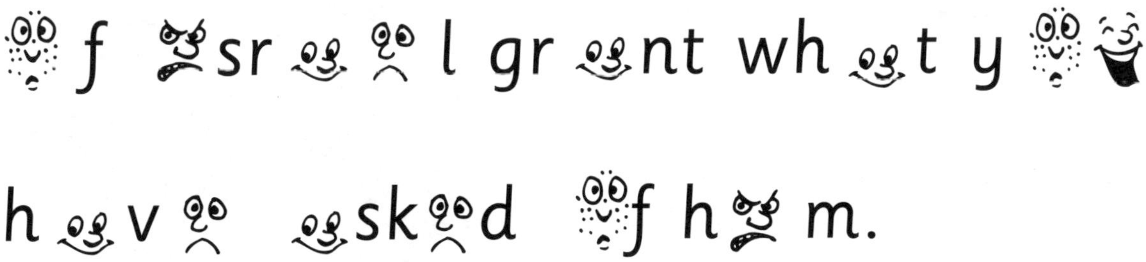

Elkanah took his family home and one day Hannah had some wonderful news. She was pregnant. Eventually she gave birth to a son, and called him Samuel. Hannah's heart rejoiced in the LORD. In the wordsearch below, find all the names mentioned in the story so far. Click says there is an extra puzzle for us to do. Write out the leftover letters in the spaces below to find out why Hannah named her little boy Samuel.

E	P	E	N	I	N	N	A	H	B
E	L	S	A	H	E	N	I	H	P
C	A	K	U	H	A	N	N	A	H
S	E	E	A	S	A	M	U	E	L
I	L	A	S	N	K	E	D	T	H
E	I	L	O	R	A	D	F	O	R
H	O	P	H	N	I	H	H	I	M

_ _ _ _ _ _ _   _   _ _ _ _ _   _ _ _   _ _ _ _   _ _ _   _ _ _   1 SAMUEL 1:20

EXTRA EXTRA!! Hannah's heart rejoiced when she realised she was expecting a baby. In Luke 1:47 another woman rejoices over a very special child. This child was Jesus Christ, the Saviour. Look up the Bible verse to find out who the woman was. Romans 5:11 gives us one reason to rejoice. It says, "Not only is this so, but we also rejoice in God through our Lord Jesus Christ, through whom we have now received reconciliation."

2. Hophni and Phinehas

During this time in the land of Israel many people were going against God's commands. Even the highest in the land were turning away from the one true God. Harry, can you tell us about some of these Bible baddies?

Sure, look at these two: Hophni and Phinehas. They were Eli's sons. They should have known better. They worked in the temple, but they did not love God, even though they were priests! They abused their power in order to get their own way. People would bring sacrifices to the tabernacle, but Hophni and Phinehas took these sacrifices for themselves. Some women who worked there were treated badly by the two men. Hophni and Phinehas cared nothing for God's special place of worship. What did God think about this? Well, Click has downloaded a puzzle to help you find out. The key for the code is below.

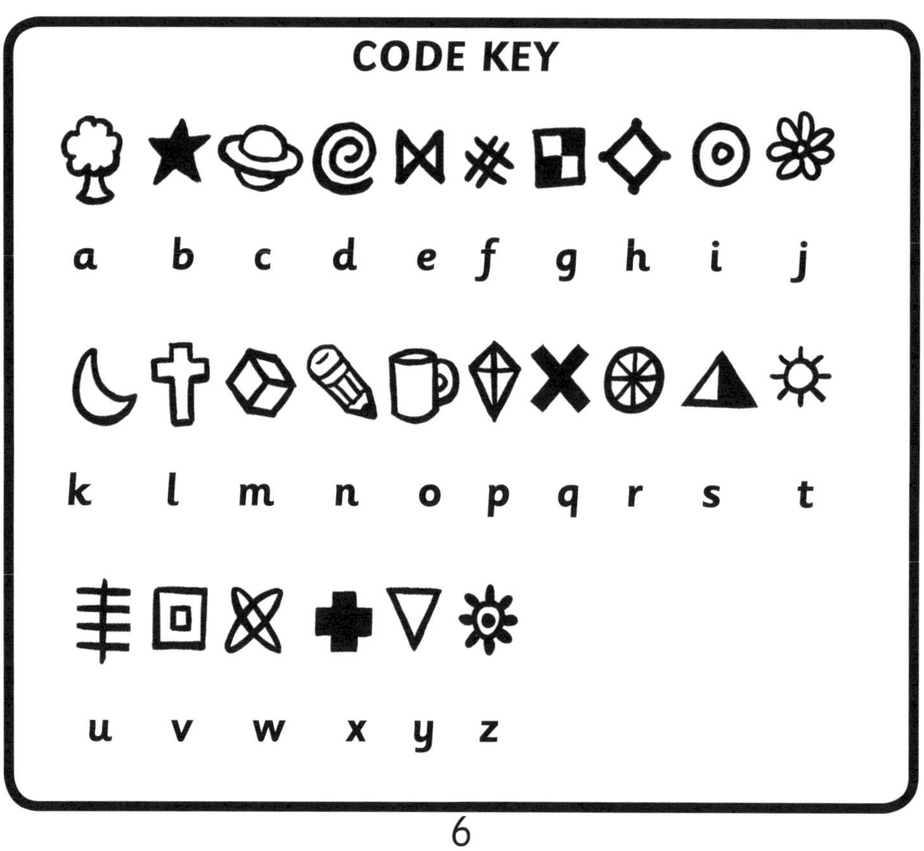

When Eli heard about these things he spoke to them. Follow the arrows in the puzzle below to see what he said.

A man of God then came to Eli with a message from the LORD. His family would suffer from the LORD's judgement because of Hophni and Phinehas. Both sons would die on the same day and no man in their family line would ever live to old age. But at this very same time there was a young child being looked after by his mother, Hannah. We haven't forgotten about Samuel. Use the same code from the previous page to help you find out more about him.

1 SAMUEL 2:26

3. The LORD calls Samuel

Is there any more information about Samuel's childhood, Harry?

Yes. Click and I have brought up the next Bible chapter. It's an amazing story. While Samuel was still quite young his mother took him to live at the tabernacle in Shiloh. He was old enough to live away from home, so Hannah kept her promise to give her child to God. She gave him to Eli to look after and train. Samuel was to grow up in the tabernacle serving God. But one night something happened that would change Samuel's life forever ... someone spoke to him. Samuel thought it was Eli and ran to him and said, "Here I am. You called me." But Eli was not the one who had spoken. He told him to go back and lie down. The second time it happened, Samuel still thought it must be Eli, but it was not. To find out what happened next write the words from the jigsaw pieces into the completed puzzle by matching the shapes. Then you will be able to read that bit of the story in order.

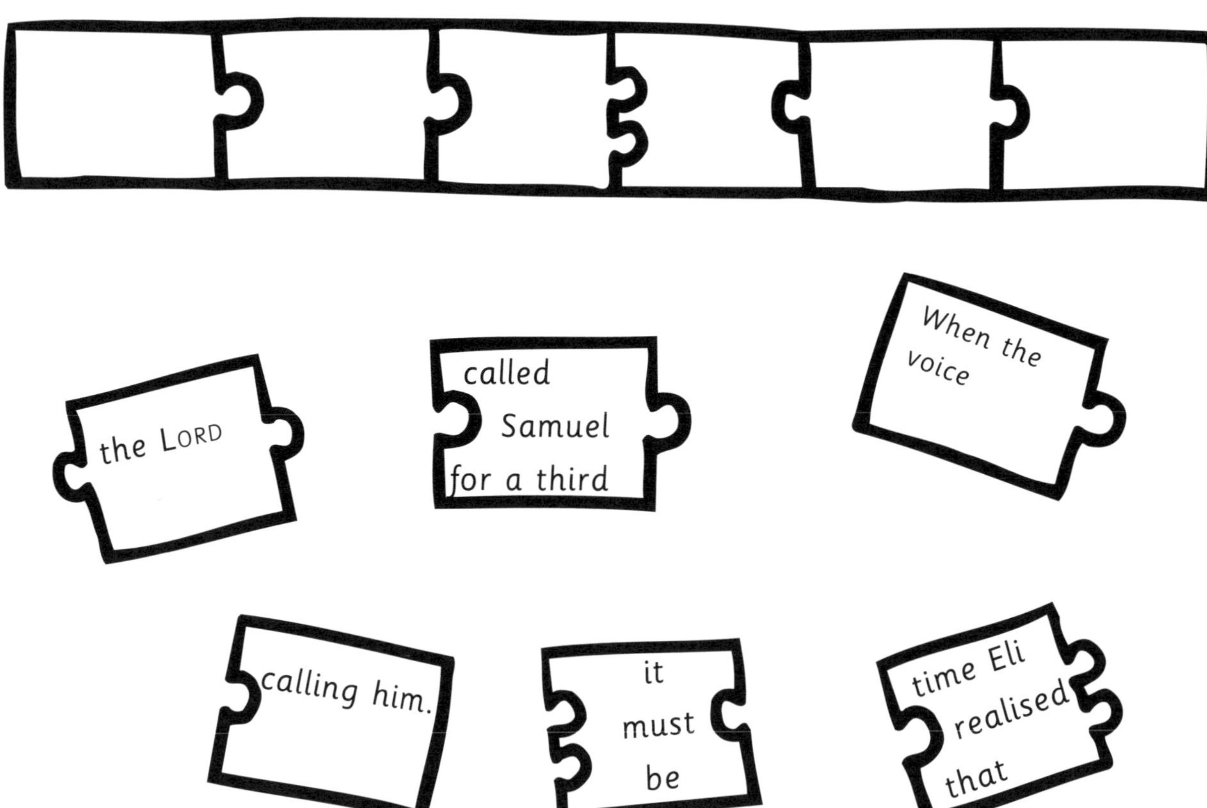

Using the clocks you can discover what Eli told Samuel to do this time.

6 am 2pm, 12 am 1 pm 3 am, 11 am 8 am 4 am, 3 am 2 pm 10 pm 1 pm,

12 am 1 pm 3 am, 8 am 5 am, 7 am 4 am, 2 am 12 am 11 am 11 am 6 pm,

11 pm 2 pm 8 pm, 6 pm 12 am 11 pm, 6 pm 3 pm 4 am 12 am 10 am,

11 am 2 pm 5 pm 3 am, 5 am 2pm 5pm, 11 pm 2 pm 8 pm 5 pm,

6 pm 4 am 5 pm 9 pm 12 am 1 pm 7 pm, 8 am 6 pm,

11 am 8 am 6 pm 7 pm 4 am 1 pm 8 am 1 pm 6 am.

This is just what happened. When the LORD called again, Samuel answered him and the LORD spoke to him. Samuel was told how God would judge Eli's family and that what God had spoken would be carried out.

Fill in the blanks with the words on the list:

Samuel	afraid
God	hide
everything	Eli

Samuel was _ _ _ _ _ _ _ to tell Eli what _ _ _ had said. _ _ _ asked

“Do not _ _ _ _ it from me.” So _ _ _ _ _ _ _ told him

_ _ _ _ _ _ _ _ _ _ _ _ .

Can you work out what Eli said next?

Use the first letter of each picture to decode the message.

_ _

_ _ _ _ _ _ _ _ _ _ _ _ _

_ _ _ _ _ _ _ _ . 1 Samuel 3:18

God was with Samuel and Samuel’s words came to all Israel.

4. Hophni and Phinehas

But what happened to Hophni and Phinehas, Jess? Can we find out anything more about them?

Yes! Apparently there was a battle between Israel and their enemy, the Philistines. Israel lost. The Israelite soldiers went back to their tents to talk about their defeat. They asked, "Why did God let us lose?" They thought that there might be a chance of winning if they tried once more, but this time they'd bring the Ark of the Covenant with them. They planned to bring it into battle to see if they would have victory. Check out the Bible fact to find out about the Ark of the Covenant.

Bible Fact: The Ark of the Covenant was the special box that God told Moses to build. It was kept in the tabernacle and later in the temple in the Holy of Holies.

Hophni and Phinehas went to Shiloh to collect the Ark. When the Ark arrived the people made a great noise which frightened the Philistines. They had heard about the Israelites' God. The Philistines fought hard and the Israelites were defeated again. Israel lost thirty thousand men, the Ark of the Covenant was captured and Eli's two sons died. This was a terrible day for Israel. A man ran back to the temple at Shiloh with the news from the battlefield.

His clothes were torn and dust was on his head. When he arrived, there was Eli sitting on his chair by the side of the road, watching. He wanted to know about the Ark of the Covenant. When the man entered the town and told what had happened, the whole town sent up a cry. Eli heard the commotion and asked, "What is the meaning of this uproar?"

Turn over the page. Click has downloaded a puzzle for us to do. When we complete it, we will find out what Eli was told.

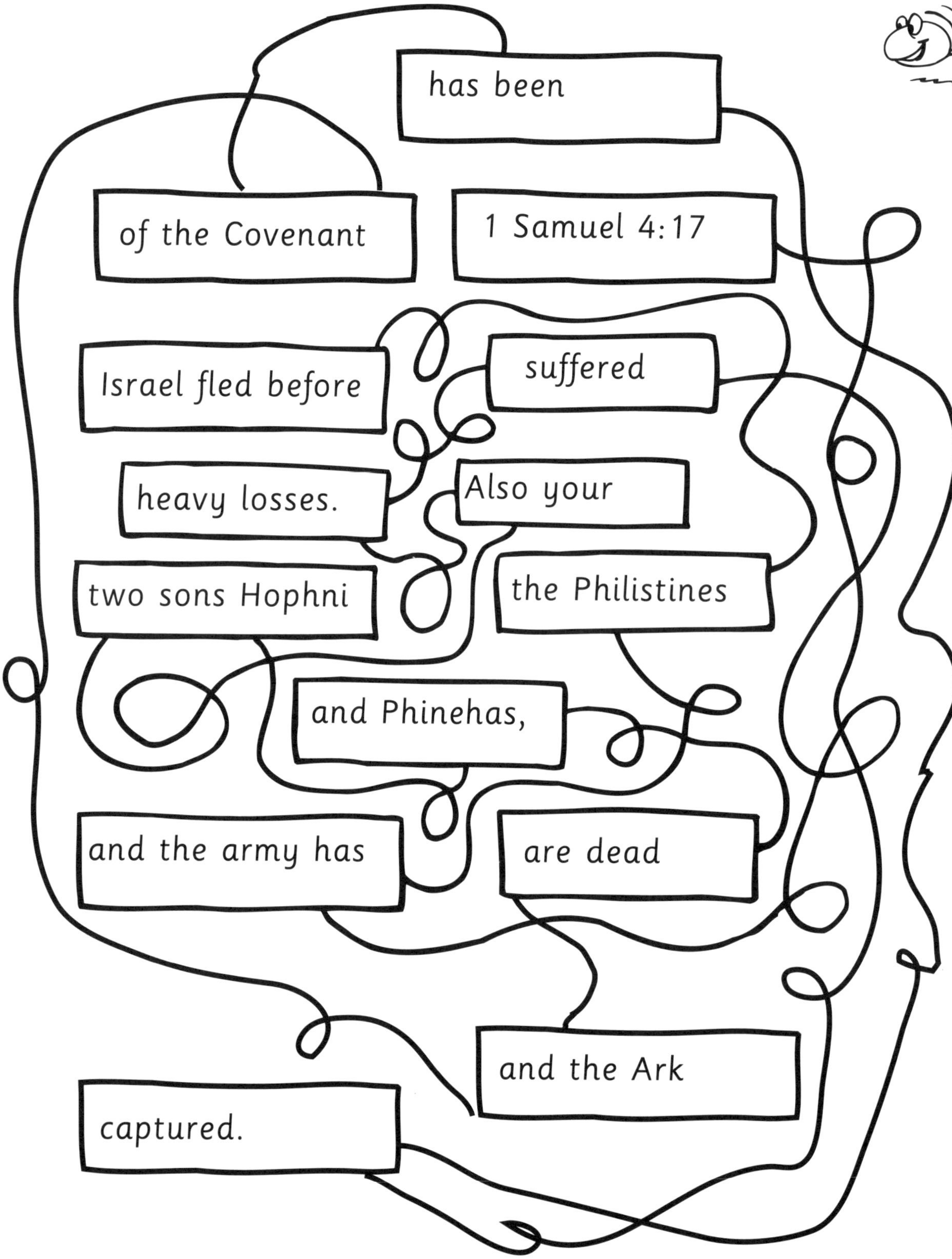

What happened next? Look in the mirror to find out.

Eli fell backwards
off his chair and died.

5. The Ark of the Covenant

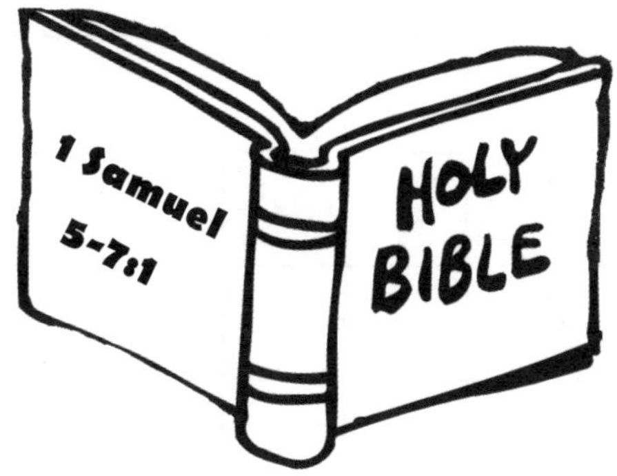

Click has found out that the Philistines took the Ark of the Covenant to a place called Ashdod where they kept it in the temple of their false god, Dagon. But in the morning, when the people went into the temple, Dagon had fallen face down before the Ark. And it wasn't just an accident, because after they had put Dagon back, the next day he fell on his face again with his hands and head broken off. The one true God was victorious. The Philistines were worried, so the Ark was moved. It went to Gath and then to Ekron. But everywhere it went the hand of God was heavy on the people, lots got sick and died. So the Ark of God was sent back to Israel on a cart. Now here's another puzzle. Can you spot the six differences between these two pictures?

Once you've answered the following questions there is a grid over the page to put the answers in. Some of the letters have been put in already to help you out. The answers to the questions are all from 1 Samuel. Just look up the references.

1. What was returned? 6:1
2. Where was it brought to? 6:13
3. Whose field were they working in? 6:14
4. What did they do to the wood of the cart? 6:14
5. What happened to the cows? 6:14
6. What was placed along with the Ark on a large rock? 6:15
7. What happened to seventy of the men who looked into the Ark? 6:19
8. The Ark was then taken to whose house? 7:1

1										**k**													
2											**h**												
3														**a**									
4							**c**																
5								**r**															
6													**t**										
7							**d**																
8					**b**																		

Fit the answers in the grid. Some of the letters have been put in already to help you out. The column of boxes underneath the arrow will tell us what the Israelites first response was when they saw the ark return.

EXTRA EXTRA!! Isn't it amazing that the one true God was victorious. Jesus Christ was victorious too. Some people think that he was a victim when he died on the cross. But the Bible tells us that he chose to die. He gave up his spirit. And when he died he completed the mission that God the Father had given him. It was Jesus' death that purchased forgiveness of sins for his people, for those who trust in him to save them from their sin.

6. Samuel Grows Up

So what happened to Samuel when he was grown-up? One day he was preaching to the Israelites. He explained that if the people returned to God, got rid of their false gods and served God only, God would deliver them out of the hands of the Philistines. Because Samuel was a prophet he prayed to God to show mercy to the people. The Israelites were told to assemble at Mizpah and Samuel prayed for them. Decode the Israelites' confession.

VD GZUD RHMMDC ZFZHMRS SGD KNQC.

A=B	B=C	C=D	D=E	E=F	F=G	G=H	H=I
I=J	J=K	K=L	L=M	M=N	N=O	O=P	P=Q
Q=R	R=S	S=T	T=U	U=V	V=W	W=X	X=Y
Y=Z	Z=A						

_ _   _ _ _ _   _ _ _ _ _ _ _

_ _ _ _ _ _ _   _ _ _   _ _ _ _.

The Philistines heard that the Israelites were all together at Mizpah. They thought this would be an excellent opportunity to fight them. When the Israelites heard that the Philistines were going to attack, they were very afraid. They asked Samuel to ask God for help, the LORD answered him.

EXTRA EXTRA!! God showed mercy to the people of Israel. The Bible tells us that God is the same yesterday today and forever. He has shown mercy many times throughout the years – most importantly when he gave his Son Jesus Christ to save sinners. John 3:16 tells us that God so loved the world that he gave his one and only Son so that whoever believes in him should not perish but have eternal life.

To find out what happened next, unjumble the words below and fit them into the gaps in the following sentence.

The LORD sent _ _ _ _ _ _ _ and the _ _ _ _ _ _ _ _ _ _ _ panicked. The Israelites rushed out to _ _ _ _ _ _ them and _ _ _ _ _ _ many of them as they tried to run away.

HREDNUT STSEINILHPI PSRUEU DLLEIK

Samuel's message to the Israelites was encouraging. Find out what it is by holding this message up to a mirror.

After that the Philistines were subdued and did not invade the Israelite territory again.

Throughout Samuel's lifetime God's hand was heavy against the Philistines. To find out what territory was returned to Israelite control crack the alphabet code below by taking the first letter of each object.

_ _

7. Israel wants a King

Click has found a maze puzzle for us. Follow the path to learn more about the next chapter in the Bible.

Write out the following letters backwards to read what God said.

GNIK A MEHT EVIG DNA MEHT OT NETSIL ← (Start here)

_ _ _ _ _ _   _ _   _ _ _ _   _ _ _   _ _ _ _   _ _ _ _

_   _ _ _ _

8. The First King of Israel

So who became the Israelite king? Well, God had a plan of how to provide for his people. Let's meet Saul.

This is some basic information about Saul and what he was like. How about doing a picture of yourself and putting some similar facts about you beside it. How would you describe yourself? Saul sounds quite a good man to know - he's from a good family, physically he's in good shape. But we'll find out more about Saul and what he was really like later on. For now let's find out about the first time that Samuel met Saul. Saul had a problem. He had lost something. What had he lost? To find out, crack the following code.

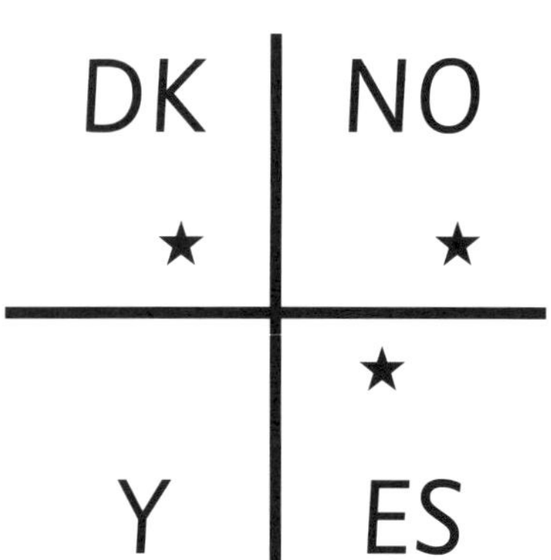

On the next page Click has downloaded a puzzle for us to complete. It's the story about how Saul solved the problem of his missing donkeys but there are words missing. To find the missing words you have to crack the code. Each number stands for a letter of the alphabet - but what? See if you can work it out.

One day Kish's donkeys went 13, 9, 19, 19, 9, 14, 7, he sent his son Saul and a 19, 5, 18, 22, 1, 14, 20 to look for them. They couldn't find them so Saul suggested they go 8, 15, 13, 5. The servant suggested that perhaps 19, 1, 13, 21, 5, 12 could help them find the donkeys. They decided to 20, 18, 1, 22, 5, 12 to where Samuel was. Before they arrived God spoke to Samuel. "About this time 20, 15, 13, 15, 18, 18, 15, 23 I will send you a man from the land of 2, 5, 14, 10, 1, 13, 9, 14. Anoint him 18, 21, 12, 5, 18 over my people Israel; he will 4, 5, 12, 9, 22, 5, 18 my people from the hand of the 16, 8, 9, 12, 9, 19, 20, 9, 14, 5, 19." As 19, 1, 21, 12 arrived, 19, 1, 13, 21, 5, 12 caught sight of him and the LORD told him that this was the 13, 1, 14. Samuel anointed Saul with 15, 9, 12 in private and told him that he would be leader. Samuel told him about 20, 8, 18, 5, 5 sets of people he would 13, 5, 5, 20 that day – these 16, 18, 15, 16, 8, 5, 3, 9, 5, 19 came true. The last group of people he met were 16, 18, 15, 16, 8, 5, 20, 19. The 19, 16, 9, 18, 9, 20 of the LORD came upon Saul in 16, 15, 23, 5, 18, he prophesied with the prophets and became a 3, 8, 1, 14, 7, 5, 4 man. Saul was God's chosen one to be king.

Harry, look at this. I've found another puzzle for the Bible Detectives to do. This time it's a word search. Let's see if they can find all the words listed below in the wordsearch grid!

L	E	A	D	E	R	L	U	A	S
G	O	P	O	U	R	E	D	E	A
T	N	I	S	R	A	E	L	Z	M
I	X	I	Y	A	T	U	C	Y	U
R	P	T	K	N	Q	A	H	E	E
I	U	S	I	G	O	D	O	K	L
P	R	O	P	H	E	T	S	N	I
S	N	L	H	S	I	K	E	O	O
A	F	O	U	N	D	L	N	D	M

Saul
Kish
Donkey
Samuel
Lost
Found
Oil
Anointed

Israel
Prophets
Spirit
Chosen
God
King
Poured
Leader

Did you manage to complete the puzzle, Bible Detectives? Let's go onto the next part of Samuel's life.

9. Saul Hides Himself

Samuel then gathered all the Israelites together and said to them that they had rejected the LORD and asked for a king. They were to present themselves before the LORD, tribe by tribe and clan by clan. Benjamin's tribe was chosen, Matri's clan was chosen, and then Saul son of Kish was chosen. But they couldn't find Saul because he was hiding among the baggage. There's a maze for you to solve on page 20. Can you help Samuel's friends to find Saul?

Q 1	W 2	E 3	R 4	T 5	Y 6	U 7	I 8	O 9	P 10
A 11	S 12	D 13	F 14	G 15	H 16	J 17	K 18	L 19	' 20
Z 21	X 22	C 23	V 24	B 25	N 26	M 27	, 28	. 29	/ 30
				SPACE 31					

Click has found a coded message that we need to decipher. If we can do this, then we'll be able to read what Samuel said to all the people. Use the keyboard to crack the code.

13, 9,   6, 9, 7,   12, 3, 3 ,   5, 16, 3,   27, 11, 26,

5, 16, 3,   19, 9, 4, 13,   16, 11, 12   23, 16, 9, 12, 3, 26?

5, 16, 3, 4, 3,   8, 12,   26, 9,   9, 26, 3   19, 8, 18, 3

16, 8, 27,   11, 27, 9, 26, 15,   11, 19, 19,   5, 16, 3,   10, 3, 9, 10, 19, 3.

Then the Israelites all went home. Some godly men went with Saul, but other men were already complaining. "How can this fellow save us?" they said. Saul had his supporters and his critics. Some of Saul's critics refused to bring him gifts. Saul didn't complain about this, however. He just kept quiet. That was a wise decision.

10. Saul's First Battle

Let's find out how Saul got on during his first battle as King of Israel. Some Israelites were being threatened by the Ammonites, so they sent out a messenger to see if any other Israelites could help them. Saul rose to the challenge. Use the clock to crack the code and find out what happened.

7 p.m. 7 a.m. 4 a.m., 6 p.m. 3 p.m. 8 a.m. 5 p.m. 8 a.m. 7 p.m.,

2 p.m. 5a.m., 6 a.m. 2 p.m. 3 a.m., 2 a.m., 12 a.m. 12 p.m. 4 a.m.,

8 p.m. 3 p.m. 2 p.m., 1 p.m., 7 a.m. 8 a.m. 12 p.m., 8 a.m. 1 p.m.,

3 p.m. 2 p.m. 10 p.m. 4 a.m. 5 p.m., 12 a.m. 1 p.m. 3 a.m., 7 a.m. 4.am.,

1 a.m. 8 p.m. 5 p.m. 1 p.m. 4 a.m. 3 a.m., 10 p.m. 8 a.m. 7 p.m. 7.a.m.,

12 a.m. 1 p.m. 6 a.m. 4 a.m. 5 p.m.

Did he win the battle? Yes, he did. The Israelites joined together and Saul led them to attack the Ammonites. Saul was victorious. The Israelites then had a celebration, Saul was their king. After that Samuel instructed the people to go to a certain place to reaffirm Saul's kingship. Work out where this place was by following the wiggly line from Samuel and Saul to the crown. Along the way you will pick up the letters that spell out the name of the town.

What happened next, Jess?

Well, Harry, if you look at the words below you will see some words in bold that don't make sense. Take each letter and replace it with the letter that comes after it in the alphabet.

There they sacrificed **edkknvrgho needqhmfr**

before the LORD, and Saul and all the Israelites

held a great **bdkdaqzshnm**.

EXTRA EXTRA!! Read the following verse from Psalm 24. What king is being talked about here? Lift up your heads, O you gates; be lifted up, you ancient doors, that the King of glory may come in. The answer is in the next verse: Who is this King of glory? The LORD strong and mighty, the LORD mighty in battle. It is good for us to remember who really is king. There have been a lot of human kings in history, and leaders and powerful people. But it is our great God who is the ruler of the whole earth. Psalm 103 verse 19 says: The LORD has established his throne in heaven, and his kingdom rules over all. Think about who is in charge of your life. Do you trust in Jesus as your King of kings. Is he the most important person in your life? He should be.

11. A National Celebration

To mark the occasion of Saul becoming king, there was a big celebration. Did Samuel attend? Yes, he did, but he wasn't that happy. At Gilgal, Samuel gave a farewell speech. Saul was the leader of the country now. But before Saul became their ruler, Samuel wanted the Israelites to remember the LORD their God. They must follow him. Samuel hadn't wanted the people to ask for a king in the first place. God was their king. But God in his wisdom let the Israelites go their own way. Even though what the Israelites were asking for was wrong, God gave them a king because it was in his plan. Here is what Samuel said.

When Samuel gave his speech he reminded the people that it was God who appointed leaders. He warned the people that there would be consequences if they forgot the LORD their God. In order to demonstrate to the people that the LORD was the one true God, Samuel called upon God to do something amazing. It was harvest time and the whole land was hot and dry. Samuel called on God to send thunder and rain so that the Israelite people would realise they had been wrong to ask for a king.

Here's another Bible fact to read:

Bible Fact: One day another king would be crowned in Israel. His name would be David. One of his descendants would be Jesus Christ, the Son of God and Saviour of sinners.

That same day the LORD sent thunder and rain so that the people stood in awe of the LORD and of Samuel. The people all said to Samuel, "Pray to the LORD your God for your servants so that we will not die, for we have added to all our others sins the evil of asking for a king." To work out what this verse says, help Click rearrange the groups of words below.

____ ___ ____ ___ _____ ___ __________ ____

___ ____ _____ ________ ____ _____ ______

__ ___ ____ ___ ___. 1 Samuel 12:24

and serve him

consider what

faithfully

you

great things he has

Fear the LORD

done for

with all your heart

12. Saul Gets Too Proud

The Israelites had great plans for their king. He would lead them to great victories in battle. However, Saul started to get a bit too big for his boots. He thought that he would do things his way. Find the missing words in the treasure chest and you will find out what went wrong for King Saul.

One day Jonathan attacked the Philistines which made them really _ _ _ _ _ . The Philistine _ _ _ _ gathered lots of chariots and soldiers. When the Israelite men saw what was happening they were scared, many of them _ _ _, some even ran away. King _ _ _ _ had been told to wait for _ _ _ _ _ days for Samuel, before they offered _ _ _ _ _ offerings and fellowship offerings. Saul's men began to scatter, so Saul offered up the offerings without Samuel. But then Samuel arrived at _ _ _ _ _ _ .

Saul went out to _ _ _ _ _ him, but he did not receive a _ _ _ _ welcome from the old prophet. What have you _ _ _ _? Samuel demanded.

Harry, how do we find out a bit more about Jonathan and what he was like?

Well, Jess, I've got a fact file about Jonathan for us to look at. But the letters I and E are missing. Can you fill these letters into the gaps so that the words make sense?

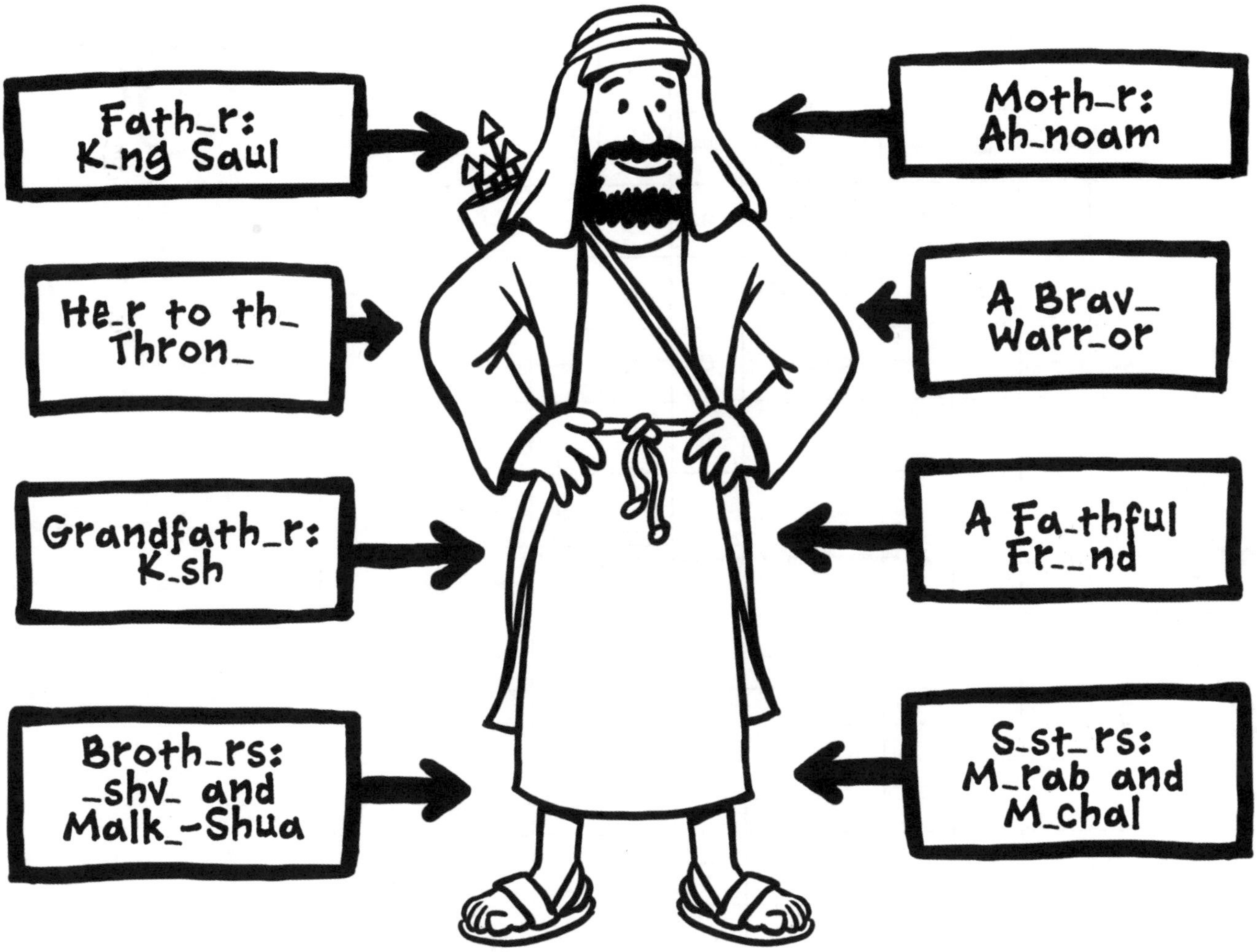

Click has downloaded another puzzle for us. Turn over the page and you will find some mixed up columns. Put the columns in the right order to find out what Saul's excuse was for his disobedience. Fill your answers in on the next page.

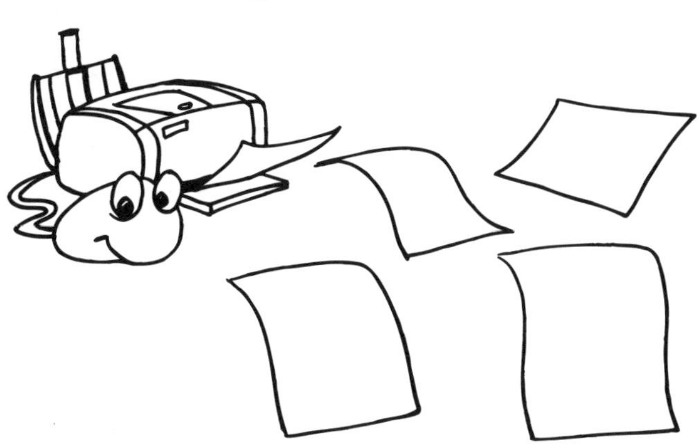

	F	K	N	P	I	M	R	X	V	H	C	Q	U	Y	S	L	A	G	W	Z	D	T	O	J	E	B
1	I		A		A	H	H		E	S	E	T	M		E	T	W		N		N		T	W		H
2	S	E	N	,	T	I	A	A	T	A	R			T	N	R	W	C	H		E	D	G	T		E
3	I	T	O	E	N	C	A		H		U		T		T		Y	D	E				M	O	D	O
4	I	A		H	,	D	T		E	E	T	A	H			N	S	M				T	T		T	E
5	S	S	E	E	N	W				I	I						P	T			L		R	E	I	H
6	B			I	N	T	M	I	,	I	S	C	H		A	A	A	L			E	S	M	G	M	S
7	H	N		H		W					O	E				O	T	T			U		T	‘	G	H
8	S	S	I	L	N	W	C	O		I	I		E	W	O		P	T	D	N	L	M	L	E	I	H
9	S			I	M	T	G	N			A	L	,	D	A	A	A	T	A		I	L	G	E	N	G
10	E		U	H	O	O				N	H	T	E		T	S	I				A	H	G	T	V	
11	S	O	’		A	R	O	L	F	F	R	S		T		U	L		E		D	I		V	’	O
12	L	T	O	F	D		R		E	E	M	E	H			O	C	L			P	T	F		E	O
13		R	G		F	N				F	R					I	B	O			N		.	E	T	U

	A	B	C	D	E	F	G	H	I	J	K	L	M	N	O	P	Q	R	S	T	U	V	W	X	Y	Z
1																										
2																										
3																										
4																										
5																										
6																										
7																										
8																										
9																										
10																										
11																										
12																										
13																										

13. Jonathan - Faithful and Brave

The Philistines didn't go into battle, but instead raided the Israelite camps. There were no weapons for the Israelites and no blacksmiths to make new ones; the Israelites had to ask the Philistines to sharpen their farm tools. Things seemed hopeless! However, Jonathan was brave and he also had faith in God. One day Jonathan and his armour bearer went to see if they could attack some Philistines. He didn't even tell his father that he was planning to do this. Jonathan had faith that God was in control whatever the outcome. To find out what Jonathan said to his young armour bearer follow the wiggly line.

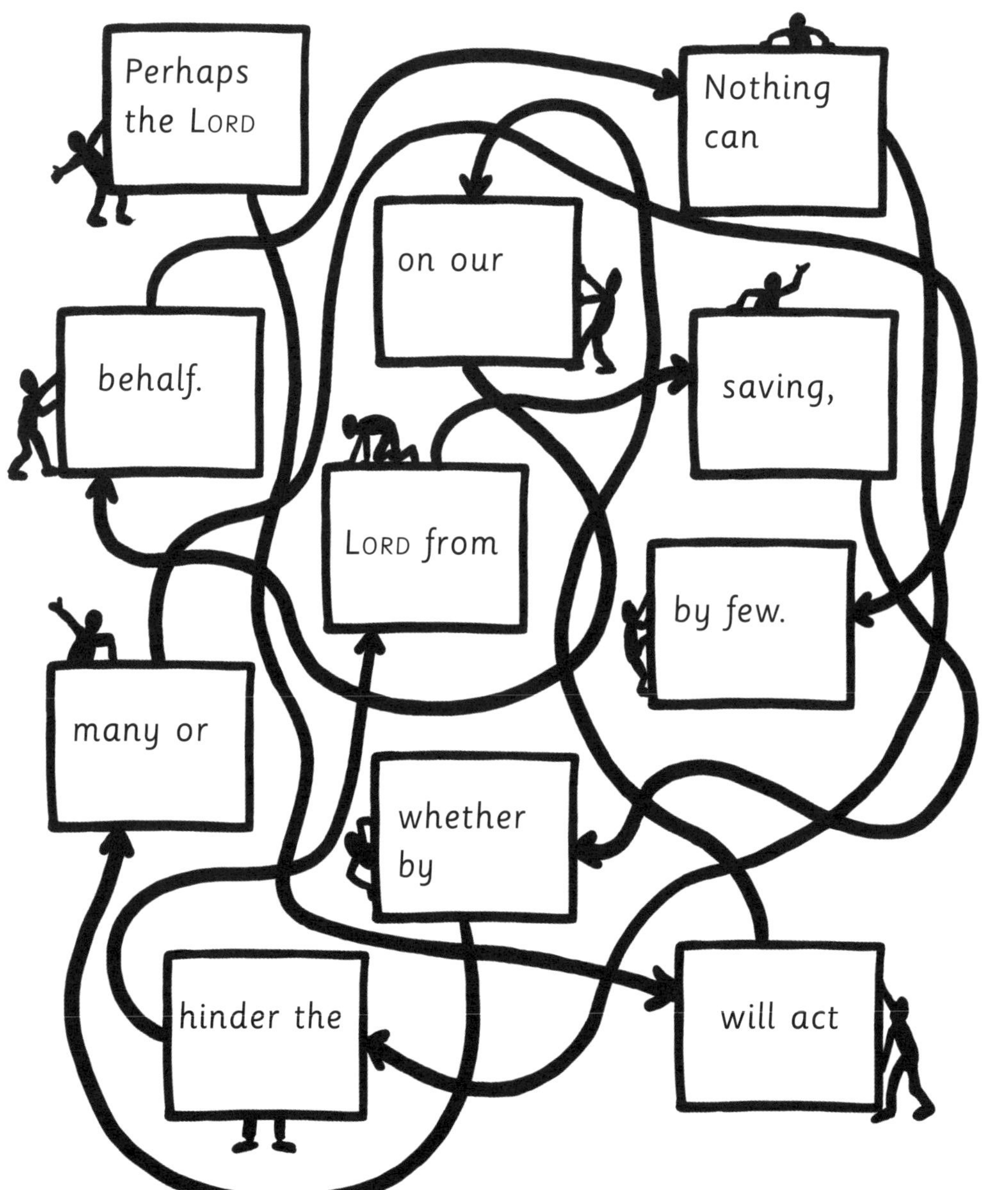

Jonathan and his armour bearer came up with a plan. At the bottom of the cliff follow the words up to the top to find out what Jonathan's plan was.

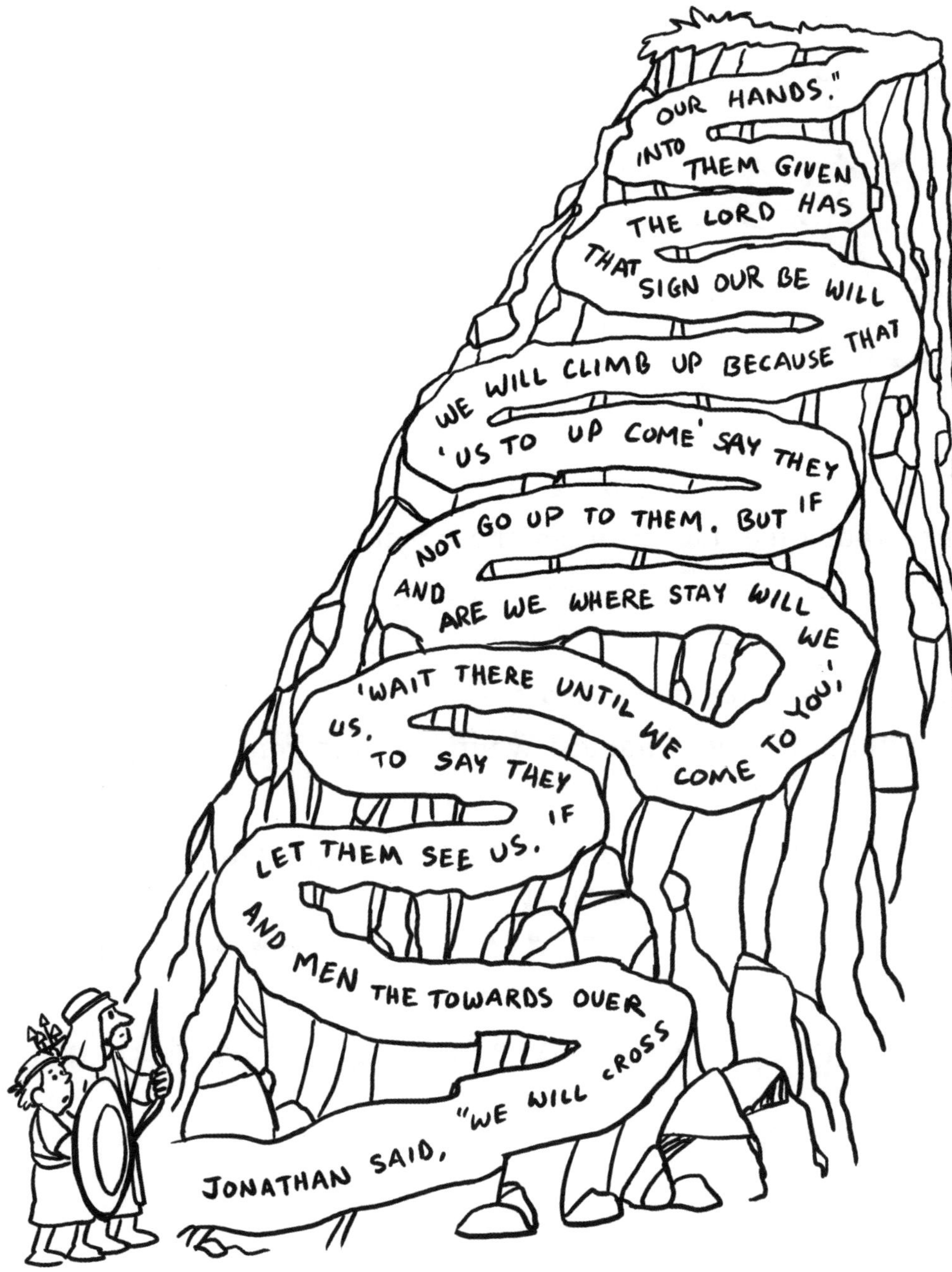

Jonathan climbed up, using his hands and feet, with his armour bearer right behind him. The Philistines fell before Jonathan, and his armour bearer followed and killed behind him. To find out what happened next insert the letters P, A or O into the gaps in the verse below.

Then _ _ nic struck the wh _ le _ rmy — th _ se in the c _m _ _ nd field, _ nd th _ se in the _ ut _ _ sts _ nd r _ iding _ _ rties — _ nd the gr _ und sh _ _ k. It w _ s _ _ _ nic sent by G _ d.

14. Weapons and Warriors

Saul's time as king was full of battles and fighting. Weapons and warriors were important to Saul and whenever he saw a mighty or brave man he would take him into his army. There were many ungodly nations who hated the land of Israel and their God. One day Samuel had a message for Saul from God regarding one of those nations – the Amalekites. Why did God choose the Amalekites, Jess?

Here's some information about that. They were being punished for the time that they had attacked the Israelites on their escape from Egypt. Saul was to go and destroy them, sparing no one. Not even animals were to be left alive. However, Saul did not obey God's command. After they ambushed the Amalekites, Saul and the army did something that was against what God had commanded them.

To find out what Saul did remove all the x's, y's and z's and insert the remaining letters in the blanks.

XSYZaXuYl sZpXaYrZeYYd AXgYaZg tZZhXeY kiXnYg aYnXd tXYhZYe bXYeZsXt oXfY tXhZe sXhYeXeZp anZd cZYaXYtYZtlXe.

_ _ _ _   _ _ _ _ _ _   _ _ _ _   _ _ _   _ _ _ _   _ _ _   _ _ _   _ _ _ _   _ _

_ _ _   _ _ _ _ _   _ _ _   _ _ _ _ _ _.

The word of the LORD came to Samuel. Put the numbered columns in the right order to see what the LORD said.

15	7	13	6	4	2	19	16	18	1	8	12	14	3	10	9	5	11	17
H	R		G	M		I	A		I	I	D	T	A	V	E		E	T
	A	U	M	E	A	G	K	N	H	D	A	L	V		E		S	I
	E	A	S	A	E				B		H	S	C	E	H	U		
O		F	D	N	U	E	M	M	T	A		R	R	A	W	E	Y	
R	S	C	A		N	D	R	E	A			A	D	O	N	H	T	I
T		U	Y		U	S	I	N	O	I	R	C	T	S	N	M	T	O

1	2	3	4	5	6	7	8	9	10	11	12	13	14	15	16	17	18	19

15. God Replaces Saul

Saul was a big disappointment. He might have looked promising at first, but he should have remembered to follow God. God had chosen who would be the next King of Israel.

Who was this new king going to be?
Look at this, Harry. Samuel was sent by God to go and anoint the one chosen to be the next King of Israel. To find out where he went next, follow Samuel's path to the house on the hill. Pick up the letters as you go and you will find the name of the village.

Once Samuel arrived he had to find a man named Jesse and his family. All of Jesse's sons were to be brought to Samuel. Samuel was very impressed when he saw the eldest of Jesse's sons, Eliab. He was certain that this young man must be God's choice for king. But God had other plans.

Take each letter and move on two letters in the alphabet to find the right one.

RFC JMPB BMCQ LMR JMMI YR RFC RFGLEQ KYL JMMIQ YR. KYL JMMIQ YR RFC MSRUYPB YNNCYPYLAC, ZSR RFC JMPB JMMIQ YR RFC FCYPR.

Samuel then had all of Jesse's sons appear before him one after the other. Each was turned down because they had not been chosen by the LORD.
"Are these all the sons you have?" Samuel asked Jesse.
"There is still the youngest," Jesse replied. "He is looking after the sheep."
Samuel told Jesse to send for him. This young man's name was David.

Complete the dot to dot and then look at the words below in a mirror to find out what Samuel did next.

The LORD said to Samuel, "Rise and anoint him, he is the one."

Click has downloaded a fact file about David. Let's have a look:

David:

Family: Son of Jesse
Job: Shepherd
Talents: Poetry and music.*
Description: Rosy complexion; Good-looking.
Relationship with God: A man after God's heart.**

*He was so good at music David was chosen to play the harp for King Saul to soothe his troubled spirit.

** David loved the LORD and trusted in him.

16. David and Goliath

At one point David spent some time away from the royal courts. It was a time of war and David was back with his father in Bethlehem. His older brothers were in King Saul's army and were fighting the Philistines at Socoh in Judah. The Philistines pitched their camp at a place called Ephes Dammim. The Israelites camped in the Valley of Elah. The Israelites were on one hill and the Philistines on another. The Philistines, however, had a special warrior, a giant named Goliath. He was a champion. Click has some information about Goliath. Here is a picture of him. He's really fierce-looking.

Home Town: Gath

Nationality: Philistine

Height: Nine feet

Goliath had some pretty impressive armour. Here is a list of what Goliath went into battle with. Can you draw a line from each bit of armour on the list to where it is in the picture of Goliath?

Bronze helmet;
Coat of scale armour,
Bronze greaves;
Bronze javelin;
Spear;
Shield and shield bearer;
Sword.

Goliath challenged the Israelites to a fight. It was to be one of their soldiers against him. Whoever won would bring victory for their side. For forty days Goliath shouted abuse at the Israelites. He was longing for a fight. David's brothers were all in the Israelite army. Their father sent David with some gifts to see if he could find out how his brothers were.

The Israelites were all scared of Goliath. But when David heard him, he offered to go and fight him. He couldn't stand a Philistine hurling abuse at God's people and insulting the name of the one true God.

Saul thought this was impossible. David was only a boy after all. But David was able to persuade Saul that he would be quite safe.

To find out what David said, replace all the funny faces with the right letters. The key for the code is below the puzzle.

a e i o u

Saul offered to lend David his armour. David prefered his sling so he went down to the stream and chose five smooth pebbles. David slung a pebble towards Goliath. It struck him on the forehead and Goliath fell flat. David had killed Goliath. Taking Goliath's sword, David went over to the dead body of the giant and cut off his head. David had faith in God and God gave him the victory.

Click has a wordsearch for us to solve, using words that we have come across in the story so far. At the end of the puzzle, once you have found all the words, write down the remaining letters in order in the gaps below, to find out a verse from the book of Psalms that talks about trusting in God. Watch out - the word WAR appears twice - but only one will give you the right answer. Choose the wrong one and you won't be able to complete the verse.

V	F	I	G	H	T	G	N	I	L	S	I
I	S	H	E	P	H	E	R	D	C	O	S
C	M	M	R	I	P	T	A	Y	O	U	R
T	R	A	W	E	A	D	R	H	Y	R	A
O	W	T	B	T	M	I	M	T	O	E	E
R	T	B	N	A	H	V	O	A	K	V	L
Y	L	A	E	E	L	A	U	I	I	I	I
E	I	R	S	O	R	D	R	L	N	L	T
G	T	D	A	T	R	R	U	O	G	E	E
S	S	T	U	O	I	N	H	G	I	D	S
P	H	I	L	I	S	T	I	N	E	S	M

Sling	Victory	David	LORD	Goliath	Stream
Saul	Pebble	War	Fight	Philistines	Israelites
Deliver	Armour	Shepherd	Giant	King	

_ _ _ _ _ _   _ _ _ _   _ _ _   _ _   _ _ _   _ _ _ _ ;

_ _ _ _ _   _ _   _ _ _. Psalm 37:5

17. Faithful Friends

After David's success in the fight against Goliath, Jonathan, King Saul's son became good friends with David. Jonathan generously gave David some gifts. To find out what these were, join the dots in the picture below. Then unjumble the words beneath and draw a line from each picture to the correct word.

TLEB, BORE, RODSW, WOB, NICUT

David became a very successful soldier and all the Israelite people were pleased with him. The women sang songs about him. What was the song they sang? Follow the dancing women to find out.

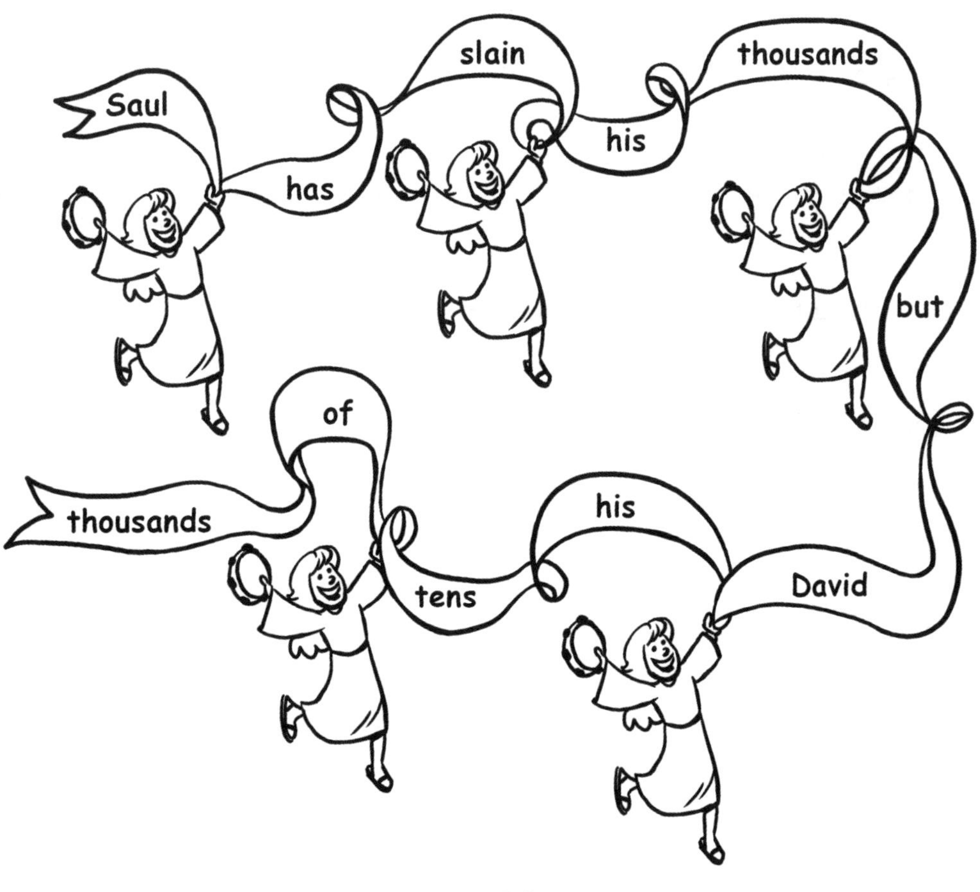

This made Saul angry, he was jealous of David. Saul tried to put David in dangerous places when at battle. Use the code to find out what happens to David.

8 a.m. 1 p.m. 4 a.m. 9 p.m. 4. am. 5 p.m. 11 p.m. 7 p.m. 7 a.m. 8 a.m. 1 p.m. 6 a.m.

7 a.m. 4 a.m. 3 a.m. 8 a.m. 3 a.m. 7 a.m. 4 a.m. 7 a.m. 12 a.m. 3 a.m.

6 a.m. 5 p.m. 4 a.m. 12 a.m. 7 p.m. 6 p.m. 8 p.m. 2 a.m. 2.am. 4 a.m. 6 p.m. 6 p.m.

1 a.m. 4 a.m. 2 a.m. 12 a.m. 8 p.m. 6 p.m. 4 a.m. 7 p.m. 7 a.m. 4 a.m.

11 a.m. 2 p.m. 5 p.m. 3 a.m. 10 p.m. 12 a.m. 6 p.m.

10 p.m. 8 a.m. 7 p.m. 7 a.m. 7 a.m. 8 a.m. 12 p.m.

1 Samuel 18:14.

18. David's Reward

As a reward for defeating Goliath, Saul gave David his daughter, Michal, as his wife. But Saul became jealous of David and things began to go wrong. Saul wanted to put David to death. Jonathan, David's close friend, pleaded with his father to keep David safe. He reminded his father of how David had risked his life fighting Goliath. Saul then agreed not to kill him. But one day when David was playing his harp for King Saul, Saul flung his spear at David, trying to pin him to the wall. But David was quick and managed to escape to his house. Saul sent guards to watch David with instructions to kill him the very next morning. However, Michal helped him escape. She made the bed look as if David was in it by using goat's hair. Then she let David down through a window. She wanted him to run for his life. When her father's men came to capture David she pointed to the bed and said, "He is ill." In order to escape from Saul, David fled to Naioth at Ramah. Can you spot the differences between these two pictures that Click has found for us?

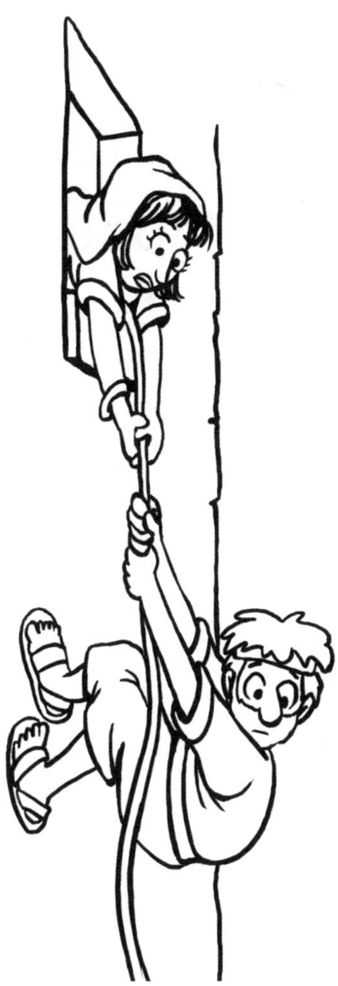

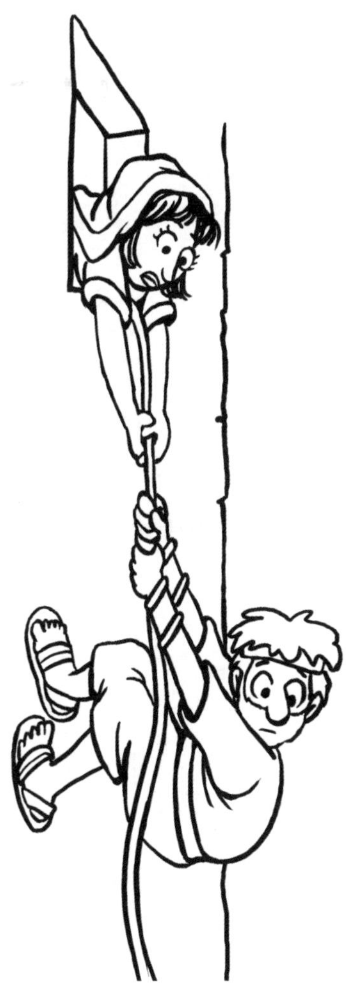

Saul's men reported back to the King that David was sick and in bed. Saul sent his men back to get David out of his bed. They discovered that they had been tricked and that David had escaped. God protected David again and again.

19. Secret Message

So what happens next? Well, when David escaped through the window he went to Jonathan to ask for help. They came up with a plan to find out if it was safe for David to return or not. It was the New Moon Festival and David was expected to dine at the King's table. David suggested that if Saul asked where he was Jonathan was to tell him that David had asked permission to go home to his father's house. If Saul didn't mind then David would know he was safe, but if Saul was angry then David would know he was in danger.

King Saul did notice David's absence and became angry. Jonathan knew for sure that Saul wanted David dead. He managed to tell David the news by a secret message they had arranged earlier. David would hide behind a rock in a field. If it was safe Jonathan would shoot his arrows and say to his servant, "Look! The arrows are on this side of you, bring them here." But, if it was not safe for David Jonathan would shoot his arrows and say to the boy...

Isn't the arrow beyond you, hurry! Go quickly! Don't stop.

Look at the mirror to read the message.

This was what Jonathan said. So David knew that he would have to flee for his life. Jonathan sent his servant back to town so that he and David could say goodbye to each other. David came and bowed down before Jonathan and they wept. Add the missing vowels to see what Jonathan then said to David.

Th_ L_rd _s w_tn_ss b_tw_ _ n
y _ _ _nd m_, _ nd b_tw_ _ n
y _ _ r d _ sc_ nd_ nts _nd my
d_ sc_nd_nts f_r_v_r.

20. David Acts the Part

What did David do next, Harry? Well, Jess, he visited Ahimelech the priest. Ahimelech wondered what David was up to, on his own with no food or weapon. David lied and said he was on a special mission from the King. Ahimelech then helped him by giving him bread and Goliath's old sword. David then fled from Saul to Achish, King of Gath. He must have been desperate to go there. Gath was Goliath's home town. King Achish's advisors recognised David and remembered that David had killed a lot of Philistines. David was afraid and thought he might be in danger, so he started to act as if he was mad by making marks on the doors of the gates and letting saliva run down his beard. Achish the King was not impressed and thought he had seen plenty mad men. So David was able to escape. Find the following words from this chapter in the wordsearch.

A	F	R	A	I	D
H	H	S	G	X	A
I	T	W	A	M	V
M	A	O	T	A	I
E	I	R	H	D	D
L	L	D	Y	A	S
E	O	Z	E	Z	A
C	G	R	X	Y	U
H	B	N	O	B	L
H	S	I	H	C	A

David
Ahimelech
Achish
Saul
Bread
Sword
Goliath
Mad
Nob
Afraid
Gath

21. David's Hideout

Let's find out where David escaped to, Jess. Do we have any information?

Yes. Click has looked out this puzzle for us to do. Crack the code and you'll find out where David went to hide from his enemies.

1 Q	2 W	3 E	4 R	5 T	6 Y	7 U	8 I	9 O	10 P
11 A	12 S	13 D	14 F	15 G	16 H	17 J	18 K	19 L	20 ;
21 Z	22 X	23 C	24 V	25 B	26 N	27 M	28 ,	29 .	30 /
				31 SPACE					

5 16 3,   23 11 24 3,   9 14,   11 13 7 19 19 11 27

_ _ _   _ _ _ _   _ _   _ _ _ _ _ _ _

When David was in this cave, his family heard he was there and joined him. Other people who were in debt or distress also came. Gad, a prophet, came to David and told him to go to Judah, so David left the cave with his men.

About this time Saul met with his officials and complained about David. He asked why his officials were not telling him anything. Saul was certain that these men were conspiring against him. One man spoke up. His name was Doeg and he told Saul how he had seen Ahimelech helping David. He was the priest that gave food and a spear to David. Well, when King Saul heard that, he sent for Ahimelech. To find out what Saul said, break the code. The first box stands for the letter a, the second for b and so on.

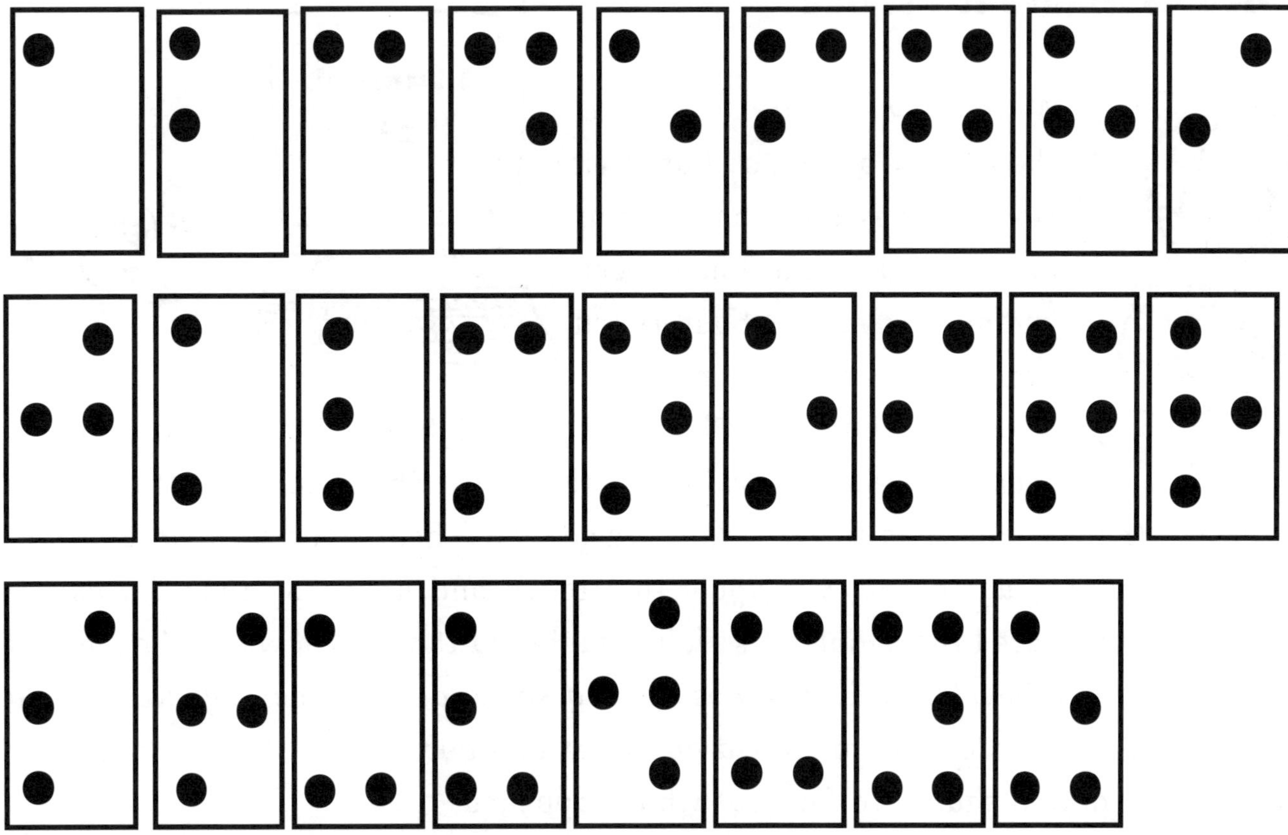

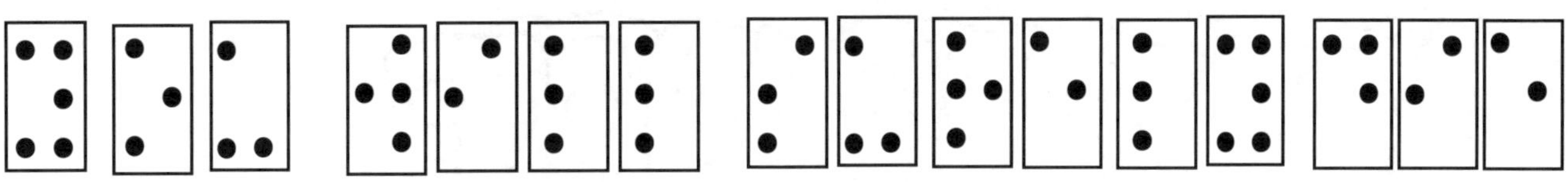

_ _ _   _ _ _ _   _ _ _ _ _ _   _ _ _

Ahimelech and 85 priests were put to death that day, along with people and animals from the town of Nob. But Abithar, a son of Ahimelech, escaped. He fled to David. David asked him to stay with him and gave a very different message from Saul's. Use the code to work out what David said to Abithar.

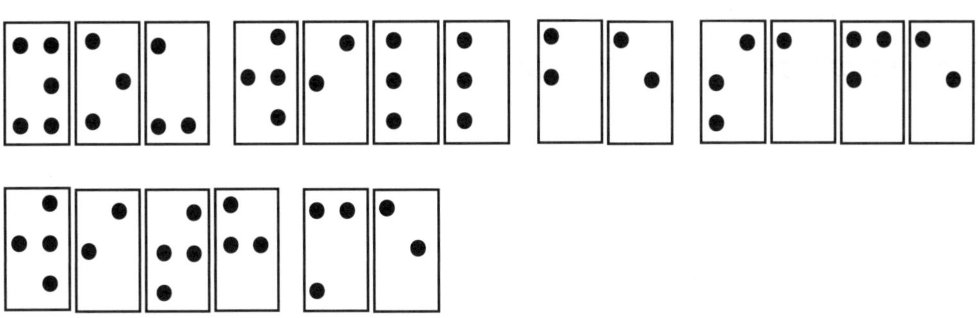

_ _ _   _ _ _ _   _ _   _ _ _ _   _ _ _ _   _ _

22. God Continued to Provide

We're now onto 1 Samuel chapter 23 and Click has even more puzzles and codes for us to solve. Harry and I have been finding out more about David and how God continued to provide for him. The Philistines were fighting and stealing from the people of Keilah. David asked the LORD, "Shall I go and attack these Philistines?" The LORD told him to go. When David's men heard this they were afraid. David asked the LORD again and was again told to go and fight. So they did as the LORD told them and saved the people of Keilah. Saul heard that David was at Keilah and went after him, but David heard Saul was coming so he and his men left Keilah and kept moving. Saul kept looking for David day after day but....

Colour in the dotted shapes to find out what happened.

David stayed in the hills at Ziph. Jonathan, Saul's son, found him and encouraged him, helping him to find strength in the LORD. While David was hiding at Ziph he wrote Psalm 54. Fill in the vowels to discover what he says.

Psalm 54

a e i o u
△ » ↗ ⮡ ↩

S△v» m», ⮡ G⮡d, by y⮡↩r n△m»; v↗nd↗c△t»

m» by y⮡↩r m↗ght. H»△r my pr△y»r, ⮡ G⮡d.

Str△ng➾rs △r➾ △tt△ck⇗ng m➾ ... m➾n w⇗th⮡↬t

r➾g△rd f⮡r G⮡d. S↬r➾ly G⮡d ⇗s my h➾lp; th➾ L⮡RD

⇗s th➾ ⮡n➾ wh⮡ s↬st△⇗ns m➾. ⇗ w⇗ll pr△⇗s➾

y⮡↬r n△m➾, ⮡ L⮡RD, f⮡r ⇗t ⇗s g⮡⮡d.

And here is another puzzle for us to tackle. In the following picture the weight-lifter is carrying a huge pile of packages. Below, there are a jumble of words in different shapes. Using these shapes to guide you, insert the words inside the shapes into the pile of packages. You will then be able to read what David said.

Saul kept pursuing David and was getting closer to catching him when a messenger came to Saul and told him that the Philistines were raiding his land. Saul had to stop pursuing David and go after the Philistines. God was in control of every detail and he kept David safe.

23. David Cuts Saul's Garment

Saul didn't wait long to try and find David again. He was told that David was now in the Desert of En Gedi. He took 3000 men and carried on his search. David was hiding in a cave with his men. Saul went into the very same cave to have a rest. David's men urged David to go and kill Saul. David wouldn't do that. He knew that Saul was God's anointed king. However, David did go and cut off a corner from Saul's robe.

Saul then went back outside. David went out of the cave and shouted at Saul. David bowed down before him and explained that he did not want to harm Saul. He showed him the piece from his robe. Saul saw this and realised that David was a more righteous man than he was. Look at the illustrations below. Can you spot the differences? Which picture is the right one?

To find out what Saul said, you will have to solve the puzzle on the next page. It is a challenge! Fill in the missing words by using the mixed up codes below, but the clues are not in order! Some clues are from previous puzzles in this book. One or two are different. And some clues are extra hard, because you will have to break them in two different ways before you solve them.

You are more _ _ _ _ _ _ _ _ _ _ _ than I. You have _ _ _ _ _ _ _ _ me _ _ _ _, but I have _ _ _ _ _ _ _ _ you _ _ _ _ _. You have just now _ _ _ _ me of the _ _ _ _ you did to me; the LORD _ _ _ _ _ _ _ _ _ _ _ me into your _ _ _ _ _, but you did not _ _ _ _ me. When a man _ _ _ _ _ his _ _ _ _ _, does he let him get away _ _ _ _ _ _ _ _ _? May the LORD reward you well for the way you _ _ _ _ _ _ _ _ me today. I know that you will surely be king and that the kingdom of Israel will be _ _ _ _ _ _ _ _ _ _ _ in your _ _ _ _ _.

sqdzsdc

2, 1, 4, 12, 25

righteous

doog

usfbufe

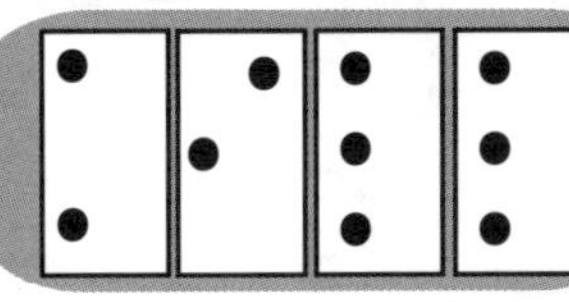

vtgcvgf

3 am, 4 am, 11 am, 8 am, 9 pm, 4 am, 5 pm 4 am 3 am

sdnif

3, 26, 3, 27, 6

n h r m d

st bl sh d

25. Abigail's Wisdom

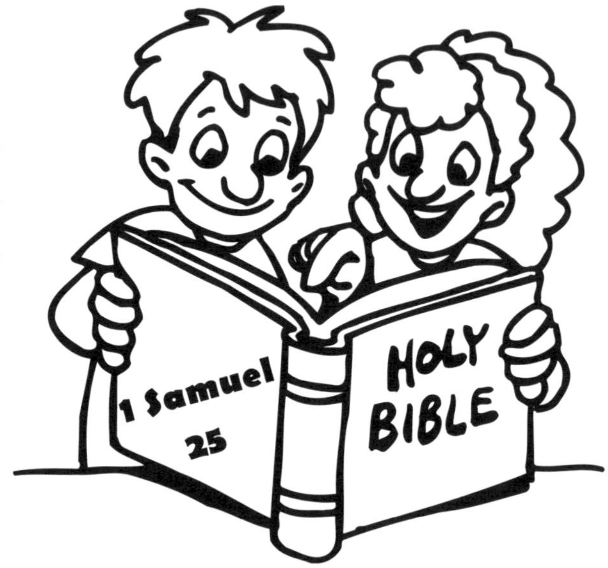

Samuel died. All Israel mourned for him and they buried him at his home in Ramah. Then David went into the Desert of Maon. There was a wealthy man there named Nabal, who was very mean, but he had a beautiful and intelligent wife called Abigail.

David's men had helped to protect Nabal's flock of sheep and servants, so David sent his men to give a greeting to Nabal and ask for some supplies. Nabal was not impressed and did not want to give them anything. David's men reported this to David. To work out what David said, match up the sword handles to their broken blades.

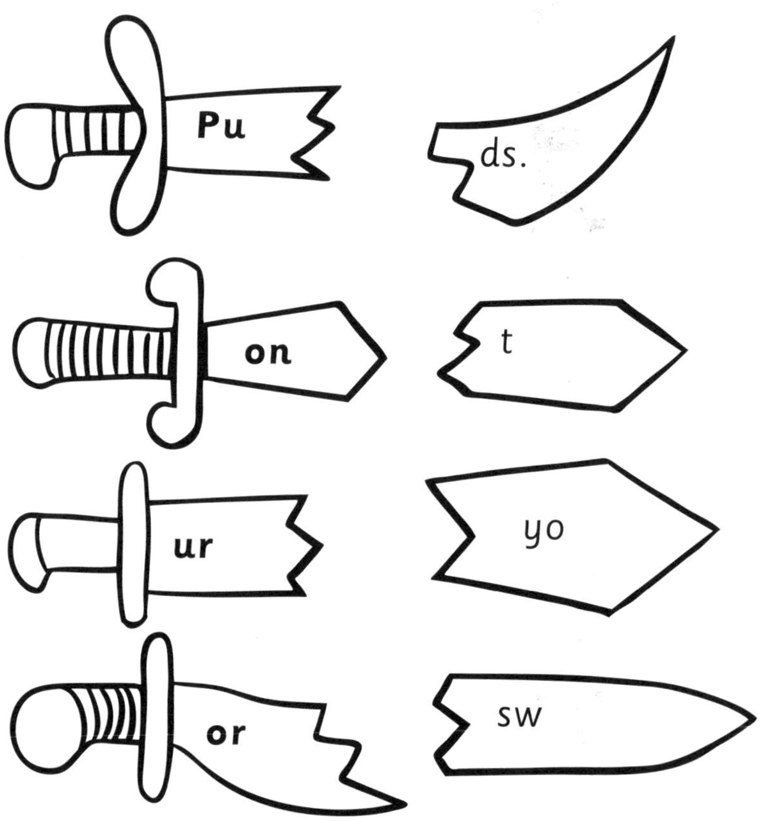

One of Nabal's servants heard how David's men had been spoken to and he went to tell everything to Abigail. She acted quickly. Fill in the vowels to see what good things she got ready for David.

Gr_ _ n ,

R_ _ s _ ns,

Br_ _ d, W_n_,

Sh_ _ p, F _ gs

Abigail was able to stop David from killing Nabal and his men. God uses people in this way to fulfill his plans and purposes. Abigail went back to Nabal and told him all that she had done and that David had been stopped from killing him. When he heard these things his heart became like stone. Ten days later the LORD struck Nabal and he died. Abigail then became David's wife.

25. The Ziphite Spies

Click has made a quick puzzle for us. Saul was given important information about how to find David. Ziphite spies have told him that he is hiding on the Hill of Hakilah. There is a spy running around and hiding in all sorts of places in this puzzle. Follow him in order to find out the story.

26. David and the Philitines

David thought to himself that one day Saul would catch him and destroy him. So he made a plan to escape to ....

The Land of the Philistines

David, his men and their families went to Achish, King of Gath, who gave David the town of Ziklag to stay in. David and his men raided Philistine towns and killed all the people at these places so that no one escaped to tell Achish what David was up to. David told Achish that he was raiding Israelites and Achish believed him. Decode the message to learn what Achish, King of Gath thought to himself about David.

This didn't happen to David, however. But something far worse did happen to King Saul. When Saul saw the Philistine army he was frightened. He asked the LORD for help, but the LORD did not answer him. Then he did something that was against God's law. He found someone who would speak to dead people.

Saul asked to speak to Samuel. Samuel told him that the LORD had turned away from him, that the LORD had torn his kingdom out of his hands and given it to David. Samuel told Saul that this was happening because of his disobedience to God. Saul and his sons would die the next day and the Israelite army would be handed to the Philistines. In Deuteronomy chapter 18 verse 12 it tells us what God thinks about consulting the dead. Look at the jigsaw on the next page and you will find out what this is.

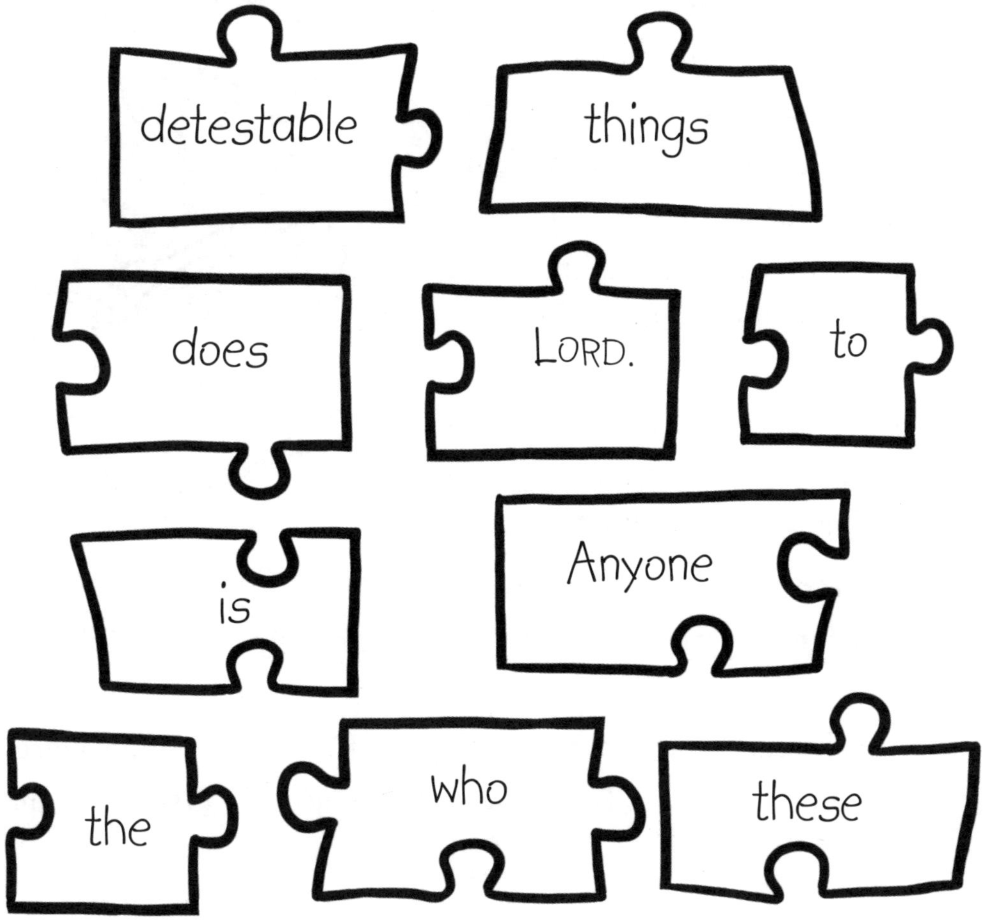

See next page for instructions to this puzzle.

29. David's Rescue Mission

In the next chapter we read that David stayed with Achish, but when the Philistines set out to fight against Israel they did not want David to fight alongside them. So they sent him back to Ziklag in case he turned against them. They remembered what a good fighter he was.

So David and his men got up early to go back to the land of the Philistines. It took David and his men three days to reach Ziklag. When they arrived, they discovered that the Amalekites had attacked, burned their homes and had taken their wives and children captive.

David and his men wept till they had no strength left. David's men were angry with him. They even talked about stoning David. David was greatly distressed but he did the right thing.

Did you see the picture of the people lifting words on the previous page? That's another puzzle that Click has found for us. Work out which words need to go into the blanks below to find out what David did.

_ _ _ _ _   _ _ _ _ _   _ _ _ _ _ _ _ _   _ _

_ _ _   _ _ _ _   _ _ _   _ _ _

David then asked direction from the LORD about what he should do next.

What happened, Jess? Did they fight the Amalekites?

Well, David and 600 men set off to find the raiders but didn't know where they would be. Two hundred men became too exhausted to carry on. They came across an Egyptian, who was a slave of an Amalekite. He had become ill and had been dumped by his master.

Click has downloaded another puzzle. Follow the arrows to join up the letters and you will see what David gave the slave.

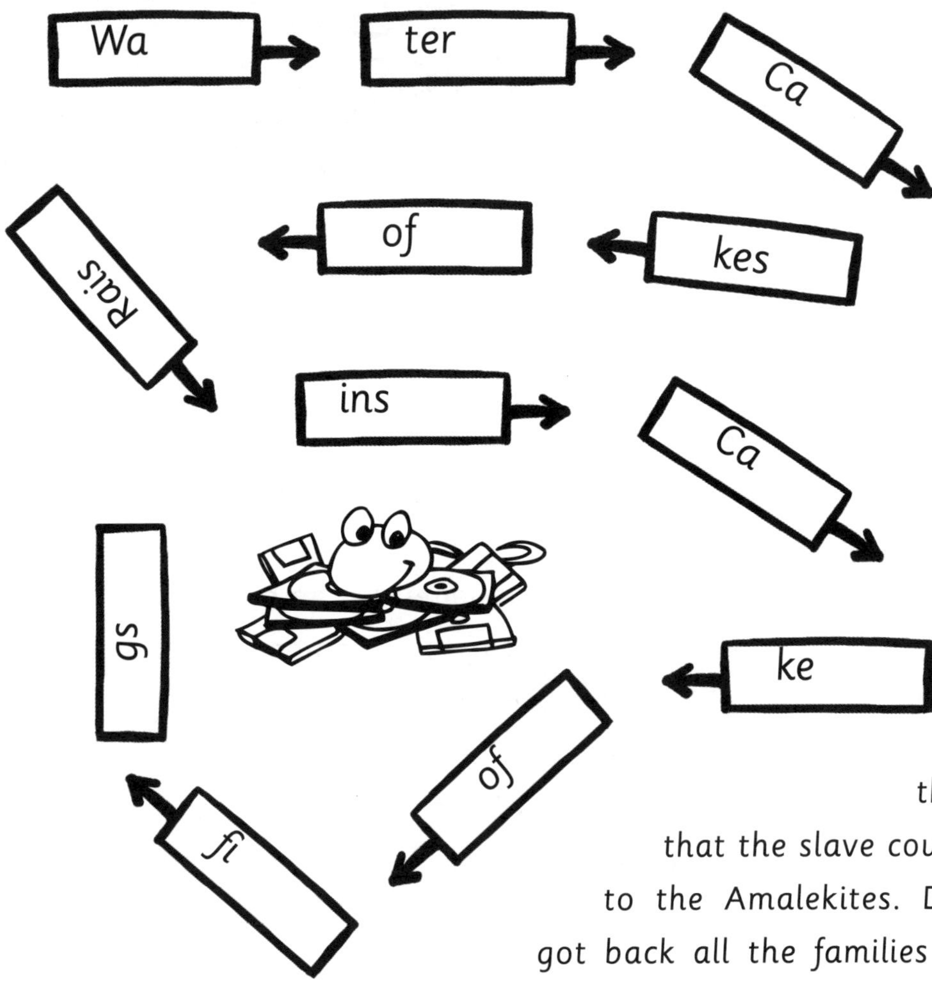

God who controls all things timed it perfectly so that the slave could help David. He led them to the Amalekites. David won the battle and got back all the families and possesions. However, when they arrived home the warriors complained that the men who had been too exhausted to fight, should not have a share of the plunder, although they could have their families back. David reminded them of something important. Use the code from page 6 to work it out.

You must not do that with what the LORD has ▚◉▣⋈✎ us.

He has ◈⊛☕☼⋈🪐☼⋈@ us... The share of the man

who ▲☼🌳▽⋈@ with the ▲丰◈◈✝◉⋈▲ is to be

the ▲🌳⬡⋈ as that of him who went down to the

★🌳☼☼✝⋈. All will ▲◇🌳⊛⋈ alike.

30. The Death of Saul

Come on. We're nearly at the end. Do you remember how Saul spoke to Samuel after he had died? Well, what Samuel said came true.

The Philistines fought against Israel, the Israelite army fled. The Philistines fought hard and killed Saul's sons, Jonathan, Abinadab and Malki-Shua. The fighting was very fierce and Saul was injured. Saul didn't want the Philistines to kill him, so he asked his armour bearer to kill him, but his armour bearer was too terrified to do it. So Saul took his own sword and fell on it. When the armour bearer saw that Saul was dead, he too fell on his own sword. What a sad ending to Saul's life. Lots of sad things happened in the book of 1 Samuel. Lots of sad things happen today too, but it is important to remember that even when bad things happen God is in control. We can trust in him. God chose David to rule the land of Israel instead of Saul. It was all part of God's plan that David would be an ancestor of the LORD Jesus Christ. Jesus Christ, God's Son, is the Saviour of sinners. Those who trust in the LORD Jesus Christ will receive something that only God can give. We have learned about Samuel the prophet and David the king, but it is Jesus Christ who has the most important message for us and he is the greatest king of all. The King of kings and the LORD of lords. It is because of Jesus and his death on the cross that sinners can receive a very special gift from God.

The Bible verse in the spiral will tell you what this gift is.

For God so loved the world that he gave his one and only son that whosoever believes in him should not perish but have everlasting life. John 3:16

ANSWERS

Page 4-5: Go in peace and may the God of Israel grant what you have asked of him. / Because I asked the LORD for him. For the wordsearch answers see page 58.
Page 6-7: The sin of the young men was very great in the LORD's sight. / Why do you do these things? It is not a good report that I hear. If a man sins against another man, God may mediate for him; but if a man sins against the LORD, who will intercede for him? / The boy Samuel continued to grow in stature and in favour with the LORD and with men.
Page 8-10: When the voice called Samuel for a third time Eli realised that it must be the LORD calling him. / Go and lie down and if he calls you say, "Speak LORD for your servant is listening." / Samuel was afraid to tell Eli what God had said. Eli asked, "Do not hide it from me." So Samuel told him everything. / He is the LORD let him do what is good in his eyes.
Page 12: Israel fled before the Philistines and the army has suffered heavy losses. Also your two sons Hophni and Phinehas are dead and the Ark of the Covenant has been captured. 1 Samuel 4:17
Eli fell backwards off his chair and died.
Page 13-14: Differences - Sun, birds in sky, cartwheel, ark decorations, horns on ox, cloud / Ark of the Covenant; Bethshemesh; Joshua's; chopped it; were sacrificed; a chest; died; Abinadab's / REJOICED
Page 15-16: We have sinned against the LORD. / thunder, Philistines, pursue, killed /Thus far has the LORD helped us. /The towns from Ekron to Gath.
Page 17: Listen to them and give them a king.
Page 18-20: Donkeys/missing, servant, home, Samuel, travel, tomorrow, Benjamin, ruler, deliver, Philistines, Saul, Samuel, man, oil, three, meet, prophecies, prophets, Spirit, power, changed.
Page 20: For word search answers see page 58.
Page 21: Do you see the man the LORD has chosen? There is no one like him among all the people.
Page 22-23: The Spirit of God came upon him in power and he burned with anger. / Gilgal / fellowship offerings, celebration.
Page 25: Fear the LORD and serve him faithfully with all your heart; consider what great things he has done for you.
Pages 26-29: angry, army, hid, Saul, seven, burnt, Gilgal, greet, warm, done / Father: King Saul; Mother: Ahinoam; Heir to the throne; A brave warrior; Grandfather: Kish; A faithful friend; Brothers: Ishvi and Malki-Shua; Sisters: Merab and Michal / When I saw that the men were scattering, and that you did not come at the set time, and that the Philistines were assembling at Micmash, I thought, 'Now the Philistines will come down against me at Gilgal, and I have not sought the LORD's favour.' So I felt compelled to offer the burnt offering.
Page 31: Then panic struck the whole army—those in the camp and field, and those in the outposts and raiding parties—and the ground shook. It was a panic sent by God.
Page 32-33: Saul spared Agag the king and the best of the sheep and cattle. / I am grieved that I have made Saul king because he has turned away from me and has not carried out my instructions.
Page 34-35: Bethlehem / The LORD does not look at the things man looks at. Man looks at the outward appearance, but the LORD looks at the heart. / The LORD said to Samuel, "Rise and anoint him, he is the one."
Page 37-38: The LORD will deliver me from the hand of this Philistine. / Commit your way to the LORD; trust in him. For word search answers see page 58.
Page 39-40: belt, robe, sword, bow, tunic / In everything he did he had great success because the LORD was with him.
Page 41: Differences - 1. bangle 2. David's wrists 3. David's sandles 4. Michal's head scarf 5. David's sleeves.
Page 42: Isn't the arrow beyond you, hurry! Go quickly! Don't stop / The LORD is witness between you and me, and between your descendants and my descendants forever.
Page 44-45: The Cave of Adullam. / You will surely die. / You will be safe with me.
Page 46-47: God did not give David into Saul's hands. / Save me, O God, by your name; vindicate me by your might. Hear my prayer, O God. Strangers are attacking me ... men without regard for God.

Page 5

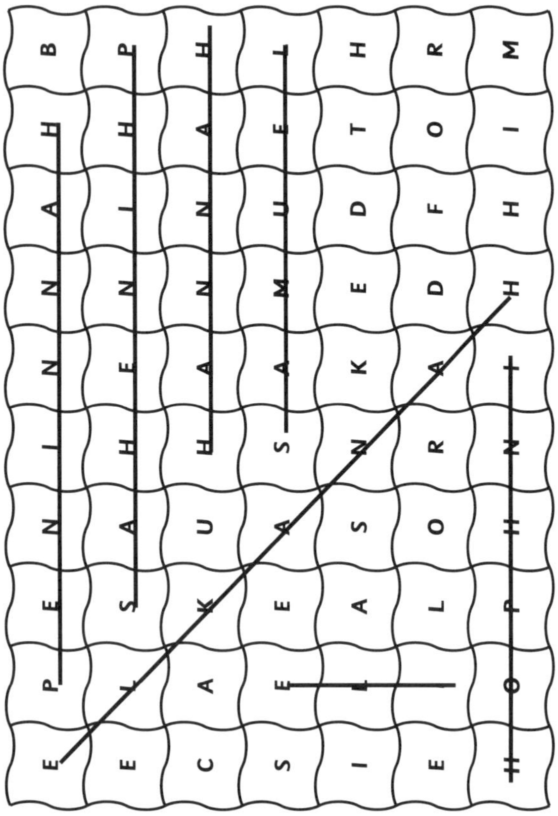

Page 20

L	E	A	D	E	R	L	U	A	S
G	O	P	O	U	R	E	D	E	A
T	N	I	S	R	A	E	L		M
I	X	I	Y	A	T	U	C	Y	U
R	P	T	K	N	Q	A	H	E	E
I	U	S	I	G	O	D	O	K	L
P	R	O	P	H	E	T	S	N	I
S	N	L	H	S	I	K	E	O	O
A	F	O	U	N	D	L	N	D	M

Page 38

V	F	I	G	H	T	G	N	I	L	S	I
I	S	H	E	P	H	E	R	D	C	O	S
C	M	M	R	I	P	T	A	Y	O	U	R
T	R	A	W	E	A	D	R	H	Y	R	A
O	W	T	P	T	M	I	M	T	O	E	E
R	T	B	N	A	H	V	O	A	K	V	L
Y	L	A	E	E	L	A	U	I	I	I	I
E	I	R	S	O	R	D	R	L	N	L	T
G	T	D	A	T	R	R	U	O	G	E	E
S	S	T	U	O	I	N	H	G	I	D	S
P	H	I	L	I	S	T	I	N	E	S	M

A	F	R	A	I	D
H	H	S	G	X	A
I	T	W	A	M	V
M	A	O	T	A	I
E	I	R	H	D	D
L	L	D	Y	A	S
E	O	Z	E	Z	A
C	G	R	X	Y	U
H	B	N	O	B	L
H	S	I	H	C	A

Page 43

Surely God is my help; the LORD is the one who sustains me. I will praise your name, O LORD, for it is good. The LORD has delivered me from all my troubles.

Page 48-49: Differences - David's hand holds a cloth; David's other hand doesn't hold a sword; Saul walks/runs; cactus missing; David's belt missing. The first picture is the right one / You are more righteous than I. You have treated me well, but I have treated you badly. You have just now told me of the good you did to me; the LORD delivered me into your hands, but you did not kill me. When a man finds his enemy, does he let him get away unharmed? May the LORD reward you well for the way you treated me today. I know that you will surely be king and that the kingdom of Israel will be established in your hands.

Page 50: Put on your swords. / Grain, Raisins, Bread, Wine, Sheep, Figs.

Page 51: David was hiding from Saul. When Saul and his men were asleep David and Abishai sneaked into Saul's camp. Abishai wanted to kill Saul. David said, "No you must not kill the LORD's anointed." David took Saul's spear and water jar, then David and Abishai ran off. David stood on a hill and shouted to Saul's commander. David showed Abner the spear and water jar. Saul heard David's voice and realised that David could have killed him, but didn't.

Page 52: The land of the Philistines / He will be my servant forever.

Page 53-54: Anyone who does these things is detestable to the LORD / David found strength in the LORD his God.

Page 55: water, cakes of raisins, cake of figs/ You must not do that with what the LORD has given us. He has protected us ... The share of the man who stayed with the supplies is to be the same as that of him who went down to the battle. All will share alike.

Page 56: For God so loved the world that he gave his one and only son that whosoever believes in him should not perish but have everlasting life. John 3:16

If you enjoyed this book you'll enjoy these ...

BIBLE WISE

Find out more about the characters in 1 Samuel. The Bible Wise series has dramatic, full colour pictures, that realisticially set the scene of what happened in Bible times. Carine Mackenzie's talent for retelling Bible stories has meant that children from all over the world have been given the opportunity to discover Jesus Christ for themselves. Carine now has over 100 different titles in print and sales of over 3 million books. She stays in Inverness, Scotland.

ISBN: Samuel-9781857921991, David-9781857921984, Jonathan-9781845502898

If you enjoyed this book you'll enjoy this ...
BIBLE DETECTIVES: THE QUIZ BOOK

Come join the Bible Detectives, Harry, Jess and Click the mouse as they negotiate the stories and pages of the Bible. These quizzes are designed for group use in kids clubs, Sunday schools and families. With material that is appropriate for a variety of ages this is a book that you will all enjoy. Get together as a group of friends, family or church to have a fun time together with the Bible Detectives Quiz book.

From the Author: "One generation will commend your works to another; they will tell of your mighty acts.' (Psalm 145:4, NIV). What a challenge it is to ensure that the next generation grow up grounded in the God's Word - knowing and following Christ wholeheartedly. It is my prayer that these books make a significant contribution in helping children to understand God's transforming Word - and so fulfill the above verse."
Ros Woodman

If you enjoyed this book you'll enjoy these ...

BIBLE DETECTIVES SERIES

What is the book of Genesis about? What does God have to say about creation and the beginning of the world? Who was Abraham? What did Rebecca do? What happened to Joseph? With the help of their computer, faxes and modems The Bible Detectives are ready to get to grips with this mystery ... but there is one important piece of equipment they need! God's Word - The Bible.

ISBN: 9781845500665

What is the book of Exodus about? What does God have to say about Pharaoh, the land of Egypt and the Israelite Slaves? Who was Moses? What did Miriam do? What happened at the Red Sea? With the help of their computer, faxes and modems The Bible Detectives are ready to get to grips with this mystery ... but there is one important piece of equipment they need! God's Word - The Bible.

ISBN: 9781845500672

Find out about the Apostle John and the things he saw when Jesus was on the earth. With this bible puzzle book you will not only discover a really exciting story but you will find out the truth of God's great plan to rescue sinners. Follow the adventures of Harry and Jess and their side-kick computer mouse, Click, as they investigate the teachings of Jesus and the stories and truths behind the gospel of John. This is an excellent church resource. A good tool for Sunday Schools and Family Bible study times.

ISBN: 9781857927597

What is the book of Acts about? What does God have to say about the early church - and about the men and women who worshipped him then? Who was Paul? Who was Peter and what did Priscilla and Aquila do? The Bible Detectives, Harry, Jess, and Click the mouse, are on the case - ready to investigate... but they need your help! Are you ready? The Bible Detectives are... but there is one important piece of equipment they need! God's word - the Bible. Help them to zone in on the answers, flick through the data and follow up the clues. Meet Eutychus who fell from a window, Silas who sang in the prison and Lydia who loved the Lord Jesus. These are all real stories about real people and the one true God.

ISBN: 9781845502232

CHRISTIAN FOCUS PUBLICATIONS

Christian Focus · Christian Heritage · CF4K · Mentor

Christian Focus Publications publishes books for adults and children under its four main imprints: Christian Focus, Christian Heritage, CF4K and Mentor. Our books reflect that God's word is reliable and Jesus is the way to know him, and live for ever with him.

Our children's publication list includes a Sunday school curriculum that covers pre-school to early teens; puzzle and activity books. We also publish personal and family devotional titles, biographies and inspirational stories that children will love.

If you are looking for quality Bible teaching for children then we have an excellent range of Bible story and age specific theological books. From pre-school to teenage fiction, we have it covered!

Find us at our web page:

www.christianfocus.com

CF4•K

Because you're never too young to know Jesus